Where Are Your Men?
Rafting Western Rivers
With The Ladies

Edited by Zan Merrill and
Nikki Naiser

First published 2024
by Z Press
Printed in the U.S.A.

ISBN 979-8-9898993-0-2 (pbk.)

ISBN 979-8-9898993-1-9 (e-book)

For more info:
WhereAreYourMen.com

*Dedicated to the men in our lives,
past and present.*

Introduction

Where are your men? We hear that question on almost every one of our ladies' trips. Our men are mostly at home. We women have taken a shine to running rivers, and our partners have other interests. So, we just go off on our own. Are there risks involved? Do we know what we're doing? Can we handle the unexpected crisis on the river, wild weather, or whatever gets thrown at us? So far, yes.

Our combined experience amounts to hundreds of years. Some of us started as guides, while others came into whitewater rafting more indirectly. Regardless, we all fell in love with the simplicity and beauty of floating western rivers. We can never get enough of watching the light shimmer and transform red rock walls or seeing the sun flicker through pines. We enjoy the peace of silently slipping by a doe and fawn drinking at the water's edge, or a robust big horn ram with a full curl watching us from a precipice.

While soaking in the beauty of our surroundings, we vigilantly read the river. We glide over ever-so-slightly submerged rocks or maneuver to stay out of an eddy, and we anticipate the sound and adrenaline rush that signal the need to navigate the next rapid. It is enough to just float, feeling the current under our boats, water pushing at the oars. Melding with the moment is what keeps us coming back to float as many rivers as we can while warm weather holds, and now – as many of us are in our sixties and seventies – while our health allows. On the river we have each other's backs. We're part of a cohesive group. Part of a whole, a piece in a puzzle. We could do this on our own, and some of us do. As independent as each of us is, we appreciate each other and the companionship, the camaraderie, and the joy of being together.

There are six of us who are part of the core group now. Martha is the oldest at seventy-seven; Nancy is seventy-five; Mel is seventy-three; I, Zan, am seventy-one; Karen is sixty-five; and Ginny is sixty-three. A couple in this group were born in the West while others migrated from around the country to live in Utah or Colorado, where we have easy access to a variety of rivers. We run all the whitewater sections of the Green from Gates of Lodore to Stillwater, and the Colorado from Ruby/Horsethief to Cataract. We run the San Juan, Dolores, Gunnison, Salt, Rio Chama, Snake, Salmon, and occasionally the Smith and Rogue. The group has evolved over the years as other women have joined us; each trip normally includes six to twelve women.

A few of the stories in this compilation are from women who only did one or a few trips. Most of them have other outdoor interests now. Thankfully, all of us who still want to run rivers do. We rue the day when someone passes on, or a health issue keeps one of us home. We want to do rivers as long as we possibly can.

With a wink we tip our bedraggled river hats to those women who went before us to run these western rivers that beckon our adventurous spirits. Georgie White was the first woman to run the Grand Canyon commercially. Her legend and influence persist. Several other women worked hard to break into the guiding business much later on the Grand Canyon, in the seventies. You can read their stories based on interviews by fellow guide Louise Teal in the book *Breaking into the Current: Boatwomen of the Grand Canyon* (University of Arizona Press, 1996). There's an engaging collection of short stories, including several contributions by women boaters, entitled *There's this River… Grand Canyon Boatman Stories* (This Earth Press, 2006). Those of us who are rafting now owe a debt of gratitude to these pioneers who helped dispel the myth that women simply couldn't row. It is because of them – their tenacity, their strength, their skill, and most of all their love of rivers – that encouraged ordinary women like us to enjoy running rivers as part of our lives. Countless others helped in this journey and there will be more. As we rigged for our latest trip on the San Juan, we ran into five 30-something women doing a ladies' trip. Raft on ladies!

You will find some similarities between others' stories and ours. The draws of wanderlust and adventure are universal. Hearts captured by the mystery and beauty of nature give birth to adventure experiences that have peaked in a post-COVID world. What sets our compilation apart? The unique combination of different voices, from Maddie's young, capricious limerick to Sandra's concise, scientific journal entries. The variety of writing styles and types of pieces, from Doreen's selection of seventeen-syllable haikus to Faye's adventures on at least forty different rivers. Because most of us are older, our stories reflect a progression and a maturation, both individually and as a collection. It is an expression of growing and aging on western rivers, of building on experiences and strengths and friendships.

Our stories are decidedly not about how well we're doing for our age or that we're "still" running rivers. We'd rather not be reminded of how old we are. We see that every time we look in a mirror. We are not ungrateful to be acknowledged or noticed, but we prefer a slightly different perspective. It's not that we're *still* doing these things, it's that we *are* doing these things.

At this very moment, women's voices – strong, independent, confident voices – are being heard all over the country. Looking at the dates of the river-related pieces referenced above – 1996 to 2006 – it's time to throw our voices into the mix. This compilation puts us and you into the current conversation and adds a unique dimension to the dialogue.

Our stories have been organized into three sections. *Just Us Gals* explains what sets ladies' trips apart from mixed-group trips. *Rites of Passage* is more introspective. *Adventures and Stories* offers an in-depth look at our experiences.

Thirty-five years have passed since our earliest ladies' river trips. We invite you along for a taste of our adventures through this compilation. Perhaps you'll get a sense of what it's like to be rafting on a multi-day, secluded, seductive, spectacular, sunlit, star-washed river trip. Perhaps you'll understand why we'd rather be there than anywhere else. Enjoy!

In an alcove on Desolation Canyon, Green River, Utah.
Left to right, top: Janette Diegel, Sandra Thorne-Brown, Paula McFarland, Shelly Andrews.
Middle: Kelly Robinson, Nancy Hess, Zan Merrill.
Bottom: Martha Hut, Karen Carver

Table of Contents

Section One:
Just Us Gals

Our Ladies' Trips
Janette Diegel

Female-focused adventure companies have come to the forefront. Beginning in the 1970s, travel companies started offering back country camping and canoe trips for women. Although our ladies' trips will never be commercial, this essay about our trips by Janette Diegel helps shed light on why women's adventures have gained popularity.

Janette is strong and resourceful. She shines in tough river conditions. Janette has been rowing and paddling rivers in the western US and Alaska for thirty-some years. She claims her primary assets are that she can get a boat down the river, has a truck, and is good at managing and cooking food for sixteen people for twenty-one days – the usual size and length of a Grand Canyon trip – without a restock. She cooked a full Thanksgiving meal on day nineteen on one trip.

A lover of all living things, Janette is a Master Gardener. When she isn't playing in the water, she hikes with her husband and her dog, plays with her horse, and uses a pottery wheel and kiln to shape mud into art. Janette also helped edit this collection.

My friend Dan asked me once, "What do you do on these 'all women' trips? Talk about your husbands? Do you have an agenda? How about guest speakers?" It makes me laugh to hear what men think about our ladies' trips.

There's a story that, when one of the women was pregnant with a boy, a vote was taken to decide if she could come on one of the trips. I wasn't there and don't know if it's true or not, but it makes great fodder when talking to men. We women are surrounded by men who know our competence, support us in our endeavors, cheer our successes, and pick us up when we fall. But ladies' river trips seem confounding to men. Not that these men question our abilities, but perhaps they are a bit jealous of the excitement of anticipation we have for an upcoming trip. Or maybe they notice how happy and centered we are when we return. Several men have tried to figure out how to be the "token man" just to see what happens on a ladies' trip. But when they come with us, it changes the dynamic somehow. It's no longer a ladies' trip. It's just not the same.

We each have our strengths. There is no judgment of worth based on individual skills. For example, I'm terrible at logistics so it's not a good idea to rely on me to decide where to camp, organize the car shuttle, or to get us back to the cars when we're done. But I can cook. I can do dishes. I can lift heavy things. I can paddle and row a boat. I have a truck and don't mind driving. I can contribute. I am not judged. All skills are considered valuable.

These river women are my heroes.

- When I was caring for my elderly mother, they provided a temporary escape to clear my mind.

- When I lost my mom, these ladies let me cry and hugged me.

- When I felt adrift, they gave me a sense of direction.

- When I felt worthless, these ladies made me feel valued.

- When I needed to hear about women who adventured together, they shared experiences of foreign travel.

- When any one of us had joys, we rejoiced.

- When any one of us had sorrows, we shared the grief and provided a soft place to land.

What makes these trips so special? It's hard to explain. But I'm honored to be invited every time. I've cried bigger tears and embraced life in deeper ways when I'm with these women.

I love each and every one.

Janette rigging her raft on a clear
mountain river in Idaho

What's Different About a Ladies' River Trip?
Martha Hut

Several husbands and uninvited men in our lives wonder why we insist on river trips that exclude men. Although some have no interest in joining us, some seem a bit envious. Martha Hut helps demystify what it is that makes our women-only trips so unique.

When she was a young woman, Martha quit her career with Eastman Kodak in Tennessee after taking a rafting trip down the Grand Canyon for a vacation. She then guided with a raft company in Colorado's Winter Park area during the big-water years of the early eighties. Martha's been on rivers ever since. In typical ski bum fashion, she held various positions from snow maker to land trust director before retiring several years ago. With her husband she has now moved closer to the desert rivers of Utah and Colorado. Her big laugh fills our camps with sound and mirth, and she seldom ends a float day without a river bath, regardless of how turbid or cold the water is. You can always find her dressed in a beautiful sarong in evenings around camp.

People always ask what's different about a ladies' river trip. Do you exchange recipes? Man bash? What do you talk about?

Actually, there is not that much that is different. We talk about our equipment, maybe offering a few suggestions about how to make it easier for a woman to row a boat. We try to bring gear that is not so heavy – no giant kitchen boxes to haul up to camp for us – and our water jugs usually aren't any bigger than three gallons. We laugh, sometimes we even sing. Very occasionally we *might* ask for a recipe if it's really, really good. Sometimes we share the title of a good river book.

We usually drink more wine than beer. On one trip, a young woman brought a lot of beer. Instead of drinking her beer, she shared our wine and at the end of the trip she had most of her beer left. She gave it to the shuttle drivers because she thought her husband wouldn't understand why she returned home with so much beer!

We rarely talk about the men, women, or children in our lives. Instead, we are in the moment: enjoying birds, wildlife, plants, scenery, and the changing light, gazing at the stars and the moonlight sliding across the canyon walls. We enjoy hiking, playing in the water, and watching the sun set and come up, just like people do on any other river trip.

We talk about the rapids coming up or the ones we just successfully navigated. We have our fun and share intense and scary stories about past river runs. Running rapids *is* scary and often someone needs extra time to scout and get her courage up. So, we try to be supportive. On my last San Juan ladies' trip, one of our participants had not boated for five years. She was nervous about running Government Rapid. But she did it – and in fine style. I was waiting at the bottom. She got out of her boat with tears running down her face. We had a good hug (hard to do with life jackets!) and we celebrated her successful run in camp that evening.

Our ladies' life on the river is a little freer than it is when men are along. We can be nonchalant about our bathing spots, and we don't have to look over our shoulders when we squat to pee. We don't have assignments when we arrive at camp, whereas on mixed trips, the trip leader often has distributed a list of who does what when you arrive at camp to ensure there are no slackers. On a ladies' trip, everyone pitches in to get the work done! No one must be told – we just do what needs to be done– usually. On one trip, there were two new women we called the Cream Sisters because they had a carton of coffee creamer in every cooler. When we stopped for the day, they immediately put on their hiking shoes and took off, oblivious to the camp chores. They were not invited to join us on any more river trips.

We always have a trip leader – the person who got the permit or organized the trip. It's up to her to make final decisions but there may be lots of input to consider before a decision is made. On one San Juan trip, Nancy was our trip leader. Campsites are pre-assigned by the BLM for Slickhorn (a camp on the San Juan) and other sites towards the end of the trip. When we arrived at Slickhorn, there was a group already in our assigned spot. Nancy pulled out her permit and the guy pulled out his. He was in the wrong campsite. Several of the ladies wanted to kick the group out. But Nancy weighed the options and diplomatically decided to let them keep the spot while we moved downstream to a seldom used campsite. We all accepted her decision. We later learned that the guy pulls this all the time and was denied a permit the next year. River karma.

We're prepared for every contingency with spare life jackets, first aid kits, throw lines, z-drag kits, spare fuel, back-up stoves (small camp stoves), float cushions, and lots of experience dealing with flipped or stuck boats, difficult landings, sketchy camps . . . whatever the river throws at us. That preparation, our experience, and knowing we are totally capable helps make adventures with our lady friends relaxing, enjoyable, and special.

Always a leader, Meeche White got us started doing ladies' trips in the mid-nineties. Back then we were in our forties. As co-founder of the National Ability Center (NAC) in Park City, Utah, Meeche obtained a grant to purchase two Hyside rafts. She thought that a good use of the boats would be to organize a group of women for a ladies' trip. Several women from the NAC were interested, and Meeche contacted Karen Carver and me to help with the rowing. She had learned to run a boat with us on the upper Colorado in the high-water years of the early eighties. Interestingly, the company we worked for out of Winter Park, Colorado, had all female guides except Carl, who fit right in with the rest of us. So, we all had experience working with mostly women in an outdoor setting.

In the early days, we ran big boats with three or four ladies in each boat, and we often had a paddle boat with several more women on board. Our first ladies' trip was on the San Juan River. Towards the end of the trip, we pulled into Slickhorn and hiked up to the pools. There was a mixed group already there. The guys were looking all around and finally asked "Where are your men?" Little did we realize that we, a bunch of ordinary women, had broken a barrier!

In addition to Meeche's boats, some of us brought our own boats. At the time I had a well-used thirteen-foot bucket boat, and another friend showed up with her husband's Udisco. Udisco boats were notorious for not holding air and needing lots of repairs. This boat was no exception. At the put-in for the San Juan, we finally discarded the Udisco's cross tubes because they were so full of holes they couldn't be patched. We loaded a cooler and dry box in their place to keep the boat from collapsing in on itself.

We called the boat "The Flat Taco" because it had to be pumped up several times a day. It got so flat near the end that I ended up towing it behind my boat, dragging it from Slickhorn to Oljeto (ten miles) to get around all the sandbars.

All our meals were communal back then. We'd cook big breakfasts with bacon and eggs, and hotcakes or French toast. We'd stop on the side of the river at lunch to set up a table and make sandwiches with all the fixin's, including chips and cookies. For dinner we'd go all out with appetizers, cocktails, a main course, and finally dessert. And we'd celebrate. We had parties for birthdays, graduations, life changing events, everything. We dressed up, had decorations, and a special group cocktail, or two, or three. Sometimes on those occasions our youngest member, Jenny, would save us. Jenny was Meeche's nine-year old daughter. Once at John's Camp on the San Juan, one of the participants lost her false teeth. Jenny recovered the teeth and got them back to the rightful owner as the rest of us partied on!

For shuttles we'd pack as much gear as we could into one vehicle. Because most women are used to organizing spaces, we were very adept at loading three boats and all our gear in the back of my husband's old three-quarter ton truck. We'd complete the chore in record time, and then three of us would ride in front. Back then we'd often drive the shuttle on our own. That is, we'd meet the rest of our group at the put-in and drop off our gear. Next a driver was selected for each vehicle, usually someone who didn't have a boat to rig, and we'd head for the take-out, which could be several hours away. All but one of the vehicles would be left there, and we'd all pile into one car or truck and make our way back to the put-in. Now we still pack as much gear as we can into each vehicle, but we can afford to pay someone to take our cars and trucks to the takeout for us, and our vehicles all seem to be a little newer than back then.

Driving the shuttles sometimes offered as much adventure as the river trips. When we were able to use Jan's family's lodge van, we could really pack it in and that's what we did on a Gunnison trip. The trip ends at a private takeout. It was a muddy mess that day and the van got stuck. We pushed. We pulled. Nothing. Finally, a couple of young guys we'd met on the river showed up. They were glad to help, and we were happy to accept their assistance to get out and get home.

Sand Wash was another tricky shuttle back then before the road was improved for oil-field access. We ran into a man at the head of the wash where it's particularly narrow and rocky. His trailer was stuck, and he'd had to unhitch it to get his truck out. We piled out of our vehicles and offered all sorts of suggestions to get him out of his predicament. He didn't seem to like any of them but did warm to the idea of getting a tow truck. Once we got into cell range, we called for one. I wonder what stories he had to tell about us gals.

As we grew older, running big heavy boats started to get difficult. Karen told us about one-person catarafts that could be paddled or rowed. They were manufactured by Jack's Plastic Welding in Aztec, NM. Then, Lauri, Jack's wife, joined us on a ladies' trip. She brought two of the smaller cats for a couple of us to try out. They were a blast and much easier to handle than our bigger rafts.

Lauri had a sister-in-law who ran a lot of rivers, including smaller rivers like the Muddy, Escalante, and Dirty Devil. Her nickname was "Low Water Nancy." As luck would have it, that next spring I ran into Nancy on Deso/Gray and invited her on my next ladies' trip. She had lots of lady river friends and lots of little boats. A whole new world opened for us. I purchased a Cutthroat – a one-person cataraft – and our transition to smaller boats was under way.

Rigging smaller boats at Sand Island for the eighty-three-mile trip down the San Juan River

How We Do It Now

Now we rarely have a big boat on a trip. We either paddle or row in our little boats. We can each haul all our own personal gear in addition to carrying some community gear like a kitchen box, roll tables, a firepan, or stove. We keep things to a minimum, but we don't give up on many luxuries. We need our ice, coffee, cocktails, and cots. We still have communal dinners starting with apps and drinks and ending with dessert. But breakfasts and lunches are simple and on our own. Of course, we still have celebrations of all sorts, but they're a little mellower now.

Thirty years later, many of us are in our seventies. Others are close behind. Time really does fly! But we don't see an end in sight. We will continue to row the enchanted western rivers until we reach our last sunset.

Martha on the Main Salmon River, Idaho

Femme Fatale
Deborah Hughes

Some of us enjoy the gift of seeing things differently and expressing our unique perspectives beautifully. Deborah Hughes has always been an artist, even though she was an accountant by trade. Deb is both a thoughtful poet and an accomplished photographer who shows her work in shops and galleries throughout southeastern Utah. Devoted to her children and grandchildren, she's an avid hiker who lives in a tiny Utah town. At home she has access to thousands of square miles of beautiful red-rock desert, her inspiration.

Listening beneath the surface –
Gravelly voice
Never quiet,
Babbling, bubbling,
She channels, floats, levitates
Inflated watercraft,
2 foot draft.

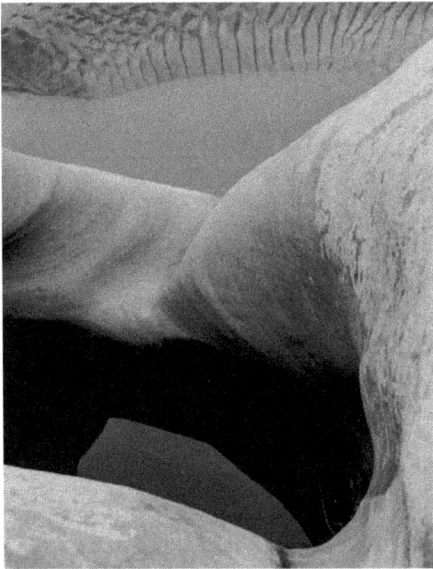

Reaching flood stage,
Cycling back
Never holding back
Her indelible current,
She moistens, envelops, laps
High water mark
20 feet above.

A search for the spring –
Divining rod –
Rarely yields her source or depth.
She disappears underground
Dark cave dwellings
2,000 years ago.

The river,
Never satisfied
To be a lake,
Composes, carves
Signatures in sandstone at
20,000 cubic feet per second

Deb, sitting next to the Colorado
in Southern Utah

Peeing Like a Girl:
An Evolutionary Tale

Nikki Naiser

Relieving oneself in the wild is something many adventure-loving women learn at a young age. To protect the fragile, desert environment, the protocol for urinating on the rivers we love takes special considerations. Nikki Naiser discusses the method she favors, and how she came to embrace it.

Despite being raised in a non-outdoorsy family in Kentucky, Nikki immersed herself in rivers and the outdoors her entire adult life. Nikki moved west to Utah at twenty, and her first river trip was on Deso in 1977. She learned whitewater canoeing on the Alpine Canyon stretch of the Snake River. Moving to Seattle for a corporate career didn't stop her from exploring wild rivers, and neither did motherhood. She's paddled rivers of all character from continuous, technical whitewater to free-flowing rain forest rivers. Nikki now lives in Bozeman, Montana, where, when she's not boating, she's hiking, backpacking, biking, writing songs, or skiing.

My Kentucky girlhood was less than refined. No cotillion or piano lessons for me. Speeding down two-lane country roads my mother would pull over for whoever needed to pee: cousins, my aunt, my grandmother . . . me. We'd take turns squatting next to the car, giggling between the open front and back doors. Like ostriches, we believed no one could see *us* if we couldn't see *them.*

Years later, the desert beauty and deep canyons of Desolation and Gray Canyons introduced me to the days- and weeks-long river adventures that captured my heart. The first river trip was enchanted by the romance of sharing an adventure with a new love interest. One evening after some cocktails and smoke, I set off to find a suitable place to pee among the desert shrubs. The late sun threw a magic glow, and I had that feeling that all was right in the world.

In the mid-seventies the conventional wisdom was to burn the toilet paper. Just as I dutifully torched the paper, a breeze came up. What started as a slow-motion realization that it was more than the toilet paper burning suddenly registered as an all-out alarm. As flame engulfed the dry vegetation, I ran as fast as I could in my flimsy flip-flops. I was horrified at what I had done and landed squarely on a prickly pear cactus as I frantically darted back to camp to tell the others. Adrenaline pumping, we formed a bucket brigade down to the river. I forgot about the spines in my foot and after nearly an hour we extinguished the fire. What remained was an acre of charred greasewood and sage. The experience left me stupid, embarrassed, and needing some river first aid.

That experience – and disgusting wads of used toilet paper that show up in the most unexpected places – caused me to jettison the idea of using toilet paper to pee on the river. Not using toilet paper for days or weeks can lead to a stinky situation. So, even before I learned from Grand Canyon rangers that "dilution is the solution to pollution," I opted to pee in the river. The river is truly mother nature's bidet.

Lots of women on the river depend on their trusty personal pee buckets, and I see their practicality for ledge camps and winter trips. But for me, peeing in the river is almost always better. I immerse my body in the river on a hot day to relieve myself, lingering to dive down into deep pools. I respond to my bladder's need and find the solace of the river, removing myself from a talkative or raucous group of friends. And I welcome my body's insistence to wake up out of a dead sleep and squat where the water meets the bank. What else would wake me and lead me down to the river in the quiet of the night?

No longer simply an inconvenience to answer nature's call, peeing in the river has become a metaphor for my life. I can choose to stay on the shore and watch the river flow by, or I can fully experience being in it. I choose the latter.

Nikki enjoying a San Juan
River trip

Women Use Finesse
Faye Coddington

In many physically demanding pursuits men have the biological advantage of greater upper body strength than most women. In this piece, Faye Coddington explains how women overcome this physical disadvantage by using artful maneuvering to handle challenging whitewater.

Faye left the San Fernando Valley after graduating high school at seventeen and never looked back. Her adventures include island hopping for a hundred miles down the Sea of Cortez in her sea kayak, sailing from Fiji to New Zealand and Australia, then rafting rivers there and wintering over in various ski towns during the off-river season. When she was close to fifty years old Faye discovered the joys of having a home and residing in one place. Faye recently retired from her career as a massage therapist. Ladies' river trips have been an inspiration that have helped keep her adventures going. Like the rest of us, she wants to keep her boat afloat as long as she can. Faye's river experience and sense of fun are a plus for every trip she's on.

My first summer of rafting was the big water year of 1983. Invited by a friend who was training to be a guide on the Tuolumne River, I was told I could come along as the bailer. Reading the brochure, I learned that the Tuolumne was "the champagne of whitewater." "Yes! I would love to go," I said, anticipating the enjoyment of a magnificent river canyon. But I spent more time looking at the floor of the raft as I lifted five-gallon buckets of ice-cold Sierra snow melt over the sides of the gray Avon tubes than I did looking at the canyon. There were no self-bailing boats in those days, so with water cascading off my head and blurring my vision I tried to win the battle of getting more water out of the boat than was rushing in with every new wave. I went through Clavey Falls on the Tuolumne three times that summer, clueless as to what the rapid actually *looked* like. I *can* tell you, however, how difficult it was to stand in the front of a moving raft with thousands of gallons of water sloshing around you while you tried to keep your balance and "BAIL!" The word still rings in my ears whenever I think of that rapid.

The next spring my friend Karen tried to talk me into going to guide school. I told her that I didn't want to be a river guide, but I would like to learn to row. "Go and you'll learn that women use finesse instead of muscling it," she advised. I went. Guide school was ridiculously fun. Because my legs were too short to reach the kick bar for the leverage I needed to row, we made a pair of "cheater bars." A couple of two-by-fours bolted onto each side of the slanted varnished wood plank rowing seat did the trick. Living at the guide house right on the river gave me an opportunity to get behind the oars often and before I knew it, I was guiding.

One of my first commercial trips was on the Wild and Scenic Rogue River in Oregon. Thrilled but nervous on day three of the trip, I was about to row the biggest rapid on the river – Blossom Bar. "This next rapid is different," I was told by the other guides. "There is a must make move at the top. It's not difficult, but you have to move from the fast-moving current, which is heading straight into the row of boulders, into the slow-moving water of the eddy. If you mess up, we could spend all day here trying to get your boat off the rocks."

Beautiful Blossom Bar Rapid on the Rogue River, Oregon

We stood and watched a raft go through the rapid and I couldn't help but notice how strong and tan the rower looked – like he belonged in that rowing seat. As the raft hit the fast-moving current, he began to row hard and then even harder. Barely escaping the doomsday line of boulders, he made it into the eddy, but he didn't make it look easy.

Scooting crab-like on my bottom down the steep terrain we had climbed up to scout the rapid, I made it back down to the river and wet my life jacket before putting it on and buckling it up slowly. It was hot, yet I was shaking. It was my turn to go. Splashing water onto the top of my head, neck, and armpits I tried to wake up from the daze I was in. I would be alone, that was the rule – no guests on a guide's first time down a new river. Someone untied my boat for me and asked if I was ready to be pushed off. I must have said "Yes."

There was hooting and cheering above on the scouting rock, and I knew a boat had made it safely through. As I floated oh-so-gently in the current, barely moving towards the green tongue that would rapidly accelerate my raft, I took slow deep breaths, and something strange happened: Time stood still. I felt the smooth ash oars in my hands, and my feet resting solidly on the cheater bars. The boulders before me looked soft, sculpted by a millennium of water passing over them. A shimmering pillow of water mounded up and rolled off the first big boulder. The water looked like liquid metal as the sun and sky reflected off the river in ribbons of light, bending, undulating, dividing the river channel. I could feel the air moving across my arms and the warmth of the sun at the same time. An osprey screeched above me and then I heard Karen's voice in my head as if she was sitting right beside me, "Women use finesse." I set up with just the right amount of angle. My stern barely missed the sneaker rock at the top of the rapid that would surely bump me straight into the faster water if I were to hit it with any momentum. Then my raft picked up speed. I felt my lower abdomen tighten and with one, two, three, four pulls on my oars, my stern hit the eddy and my bow swung around. I was where I needed to be and safely lined up for the next drop. "You finessed it!" I heard Karen say to me. "Thank you, girlfriend," I said out loud.

When I wasn't out on the river or guiding a trip, I lived at the guide house during the summers sleeping outside and enjoying coffee down by the river in the morning as I waited for the sun to find me. Afternoons I spent learning to kayak and perfect my Eskimo roll. Maneuvering through the current, pausing behind a rock in an eddy with the water rushing by on both sides, the boat began to feel like an extension of my body. In shallow water letting the current carry me, I watched the rocks pass under my boat, and it felt like I was flying. I was hooked.

Grand Canyon

It was a scary commitment, but I said yes when asked if I'd like to kayak along on an eighteen-day, two hundred twenty-five-mile trip down the Colorado River through the Grand Canyon. Once you've started floating down that river there's no way out except by boat, on foot hiking out one of the side canyons, or by helicopter for emergency evacuation. It was late summer – monsoon season. The river was flowing deep dark reddish brown from the silty runoff created by the rains. My kayak stayed tied to the back of one of the big rafts for a couple of days before I finally got the courage to practice my roll in an eddy before the first big rapid.

I settled into my newly outfitted kayak. The foam pads, soft but firm, snuggled around my hips and held me tight. I leaned forward as if to kiss the deck and then leaning even more, rolled myself over. The bottom of my boat was facing the sky and I was looking up for the light to get oriented. I saw nothing but total darkness! The sediment completely blocked the sunlight. Disoriented, I blinked and tried again, my eyes wide open. But I was in a complete, jet black, weightless, and soundless void. Confused, feeling for the surface of the water with my paddle blade, I started to panic. I wanted to climb out of my boat and into the frigid river. Now! But my hand did not let go of my paddle to pull off the spray skirt. Instead, I slowly exhaled out my nose to keep the ice-cold water from rushing up my nasal passage, then with a sweep of my paddle and snap of my hips, I was back in the sunlight with water pouring out of my bright yellow helmet. I'm pretty sure I had only been under water a short time, but it felt as if I just returned from a very long journey to the darkest place I had ever been. But there was no time to hesitate. Paddling into the current, I headed for the biggest set of waves I had ever gone into. Somehow, I managed to stay upright. I kayaked the rest of the river.

Kayaks were much, much bigger back then and because I'm a small woman I bobbed like a cork through all the rapids the Canyon had to offer. I remember being propelled across the river, as if I'd been flung from a slingshot, by a lateral wave while paddling notorious Lava Falls – the biggest rapid in the Canyon. I was so buoyant that after finishing the rapid someone noticed I hadn't even gotten wet!

I went down the Canyon six more times. Had I known what events would transpire on future trips, I may have chosen not to do another Colorado River trip.

Canyon trip number two: While I was on this trip my mother died unexpectedly. When I got off the river and called my sister, she gave me the tragic news. My siblings had called the Park Service to see if I could be reached, to no avail. My mom was already buried by the time I called home.

Canyon trip number three: On day eight I turned off my headlamp after climbing onto a large, round boulder and looked up to the stars. As my eyes adjusted to the dark, my feet began to move like a cartoon character trying to stay on top of the boulder. This can't be happening! This was impossible. The boulder was rolling! All I remember is searing pain – white pain as if a knife heated in fire has stabbed my foot and was holding it in the ground. I couldn't move. The boulder I was standing on had me pinned. Screaming as loud as humanly possible served two purposes: the vibration of my vocal cords gave me something to feel and focus on besides the searing pain; it also brought the whole camp to my rescue. Eight of my friends were able to get the boulder off my foot. The pain started to recede. Luckily the rock missed my ankle.

Flagging down a raft the next morning, we asked if there were any doctors on board. It turns out they were all orthopedic surgeons on some sort of professional gathering! An Australian doctor volunteered to come have a look at me. Upon examination he said, "She might as well stay on the trip. It's smashed up, but if it's broken and needs surgery the swelling will have to go down first. Tend to the wound and keep it elevated. If there is any sign of infection, she'll need to be airlifted out." Several people in my group were EMTs and they agreed I could stay on the trip if I wanted to. I became "Queenie Faye" with ten more days on the river. Riding on the raft, I enjoyed views of the canyon walls from a new perspective – reclining on piles of dry bags with my foot in the air. Once home, X-rays showed that my foot was broken but I did not need surgery. I was so thankful for all the loving care and support I got on that trip. It was so much better than trying to get myself home in such a compromised condition, and much more fun, too.

Canyon trip number four: It had been raining for hours by the time my friend Jane and I were trying to cross Havasu Creek to get back to our rafts, which were tied up for the day down at the river and were only accessible from the other side of the creek. We were returning along with others in our group from a day hike up beautiful Havasu Canyon, with turquoise blue water and travertine pools and falls for miles up its length. As we started our crossing the water in the creek was already rising. We were facing upstream, holding hands, when Jane stopped. Looking to her face for an answer, I immediately knew we were in danger. I looked upstream. Racing towards us, a hundred yards away, was a muddy wall of water. Havasu was flashing. We ran the best we could through the thigh deep water back to the same side we had started from. Every time I tried to stop to look back, "RUN! RUN! RUN!!!" screamed Jane, who was behind. We clambered out of the creek-bed. Our two friends Chris and Trudy were fording the creek downstream of us. When we finally stopped and turned to look, we saw people running down the creek towards the river on the other side, but Chris and Trudy were not among them. They did not make it out of the creek bed. The flash flood had taken them.

Jane and I, along with a few others in our group, spent that night huddled together in our wet clothes on a rocky ledge, unable to get back to the rafts on the other side. The creek was still too high. It didn't feel like a hardship, compared to the hour we spent not knowing if our two friends were alive. What a relief when one from our group appeared on the other side. We couldn't hear her over the thunder of the water, but she patted the top of her head giving us the OK sign and smiling. Chris and Trudy had survived. Battered, cut, scraped, and contused, they somehow managed to hold their breath and ride the raging torrent of muddy water and debris over two big drops into the main water of the Colorado. Chris was able to make it into an eddy. Trudy was flushed a quarter mile downriver before she was rescued. In telling their stories, they both reported being close to the point of giving up. We gave many thanks that they didn't, and to the powers that be that day.

Havasu Canyon during the flood that washed
Faye's companions into the Colorado River

Havasu at a normal water level with clear turquoise blue water and travertine pools

River Ponderings

Rafting and kayaking are only a small part of the reason I fell in love with rivers, forgot to have children, and chose to live like a nomad for so many years. I discovered that living outside makes me forget who I am, or rather, *who I think I am*. I feel so lucky to have spent time living in nature, not just visiting it occasionally. To be able to witness the perfection of all things and beings big and small; to experience the cycles of the sun, moon, and stars; to look forward to and relish the darkness when I wake in the night because the stars are so bright, words like eternity, infinity, and magic come to mind; to see a creek or a river and – without thinking – realize it is as important to the earth as the blood flowing through my veins is to my body; to pick up a rock – any rock – and try

26

to imagine how long it's been a rock and what that means; to know for certain it is the kingfisher's rattle or the osprey's screech before I even see the birds because they are such familiar sounds. These are the things that bring me joy. My wish is for every human being to spend enough time in nature – in a wilderness so grand and awe-inspiring – that they forget who they think they are.

As I count I realize I have been down more than forty rivers, many of them many times, including: the Kern, Mokelumne, South Fork of the American, North Fork of the American, Merced, South Fork Merced, Tuolumne, South Fork Yuba, North Fork Yuba, Box Canyon, Upper Sacramento, the Eel, Rancheria Creek, Cache Creek, Lagunitas Creek, the Trinity, Klamath, Cal Salmon, Smith, Rogue, Umpqua, White Salmon, Main Salmon, Middle Fork Salmon, Selway, South Fork Payette, North Fork Payette, Lochsa, White Sands Creek, Snake, Yampa, Green, San Juan, Colorado, White, Tatshenshini, Kicking Horse, Kootenay, Shotover, Wairoa, and The Snowy River in Australia. Alas a home, a garden, a partner, a dog, a job, a mortgage, and lack of proximity to a river has slowed the frequency of my river adventures. As I get older, I sometimes wonder how long I will be able to keep kayaking and rafting, but the deep yearning to wake up by the side of a river never goes away.

Desolation / Gray

Ten years ago, I had an opportunity and decided to do Canyon trip number five. While I was on this gloriously uneventful trip, I met my friend Zan. She invited me out to Utah for an all-women's trip on the Green River through Desolation and Gray Canyons. It would be in October when the water would be low. A couple of the Class III rapids would be boney but manageable and there would be very few people besides us. All women, easy rapids, a new experience I thought, not knowing about the revelations to come. With only a few weeks' notice I flew to Salt Lake City, where I was graciously outfitted with a Fat Cat and a small cooler full of food and drinks covered in wet burlap to help keep things cool in the desert. Spacious days of shadow and light followed – supernatural light when the October sun sits low in the sky. We floated the curves and bends of the Green River through the canyon for days before I noticed I didn't have the usual amount of adrenaline in my body that I always get from running rapids and I wasn't missing it. We walked up slot canyons that were so quiet the stillness was only broken by a trickle of water echoing between sandstone walls or by the sweet descending call of a canyon wren. We took hikes and stood before almost thousand-year-old pictographs and petroglyphs created by the native peoples from long ago. I saw only four other people besides the thirteen women in our group for the entire eight days of our trip. I was so relaxed I barely recognized my own nervous system.

One afternoon when things were feeling particularly sublime and otherworldly, I had to get out and push my boat through a shallow part of the river. I had misjudged a sandbar. We were in the afternoon shadows of the canyon walls, and I was a little cool. Not wanting to get my pants wet I took them off but by the time I got back in my boat we were back in the warm sunlight and the air felt so delicious that instead of putting my shorts back on I took off my top too. I started a trend and the others joined in the fun and took their clothes off. As air and sunshine caressed my whole being, I realized I was almost sixty years old and had never gotten the opportunity to row down the river completely naked. The lightheartedness continued through happy hour with frivolity and river stories as we set up camp and watched the god light disappear for the evening.

Some of my Utah and Colorado gals decided to come out
and do a Rogue River trip with me. The Rogue is a great
wilderness river with lots of fun whitewater. It was early
in the season and the river was at around 8,000 CFS
(cubic feet per second) as I remember. Almost everyone
was rowing Cutthroats, which are one-person catarafts
measuring only twelve feet long. Because the rivers we
had previously run together were late season trips and I
hadn't seen my companions row significant whitewater
yet, I had a nagging worry as to how they would do in
these small boats at this water level. Things were going
well until day two when Zan dropped down into a big
surging lateral wave and was over. It was not a good
place to flip. The river was narrowing and dropping at the
same time, which meant it was moving fast with
few eddies, making it a difficult place to rescue a flipped
boat and get pulled over. Somehow, though, she managed
to climb right onto to her upside-down raft, grabbed the
flip line she had previously rigged, and leaned out as far
as possible, rocking and bouncing the boat while still
going downstream in the swift current. Voila, it was right
side up! She was climbing back in her rowing seat and
gathering oars by the time I got over to her in my kayak.
As I paddled up, I heard, "Faye, I've lost my glasses. I
can't see! Tell me where the f___ing rocks are!" With a
little visual guidance Zan negotiated the next bit of rapids
and got safely into an eddy where she retrieved her
spare glasses out of her dry bag. I have never witnessed
such a perfectly executed self-rescue! The moral is:
Women use more than just finesse!

My companions were and are an amazing tribe of capable
women with the seemingly collective goal of fun, laughter,
and collaboration. I say tribe because that's what you
become when you spend river time together sharing food,
drink, rapids, hikes, chores, baths, stories, haikus,
laughter, and sometimes even tears. They helped me see
the revelation: all ladies' trips are awesome, I can do this

forever with a smaller boat, less gear, and on low water.
It's so easy!

Faye taking a photo break while
scouting a rapid

Camaraderie
Mel Zwick

When groups of women gather, they often develop a common bond that doesn't always surface in mixed groups. This is especially the case when women come together on the river. Mel Zwick describes the unique quality of women's bonds that develop on multi-day, wilderness river trips.

Mel's from back East and has been on rivers since before she was born. That may explain why she's fearless and goes headlong into just about anything the river throws at her. Mel took a decade or so hiatus from rivers, and then was invited to join a raft trip with Martha. One trip led to another and now, here she is, still rafting. Mel settled near Winter Park, Colorado, and figured out how to juggle skiing in the winter and rafting in the summer by building her own insurance business. Mel is steady as a rock and always ready to lend a helping hand on our trips. Now retired, she can spend even more time on the rivers and slopes, chasing ski and rafting trips around the globe.

"Where are your men?" I wonder, do men usually get asked, "Where are your women?" I expect not.

I have been on rivers since before I was born. My parents were avid canoeists. Given that, one could say river running is in my blood . . . or DNA. Prior to my 20s, my river experiences were in canoes. I distinctly remember my first time in a raft from Rainbow Park to Split Mountain on the Green River in 1973. The reason it made such an impression was the discovery that, unlike a canoe, rafts can easily and successfully negotiate riffles and small rapids sideways. If you float into something like that sideways in a canoe, you flip! I don't recall doing any more rafting until the early 1980s on the Westwater section of the Colorado River. That was my first time being on the river with Martha, though it was not a ladies' trip. After that, I was periodically invited on trips. Once I became the owner of an inflatable kayak and more recently a small cataraft, I was invited on more trips, both ladies' trips and otherwise.

Meeting, floating, hiking, and essentially living with the women on a river trip is interesting. It's fun and not without surprises. You get to know your fellow rafters as the onion layers gradually peel away. We each have our quirks and foibles. These are accepted, even celebrated, because in the wild we depend upon each other. Being on the river helps people to relax and let their true selves shine. We fall into river time and its predictable routine: get up, get going, enjoy the river, find a camp, get settled, sleep, and do it all over again. All the while we take time to enjoy each other, the beauty of our surroundings, and the occasional challenge. Some steadfast friendships are made that extend beyond the river, while other women are river friends, and we pick up on the next trip where we left off without skipping a beat. Regardless of the extent of the friendship, the river creates an inexplicable bond among us all.

While we're on the river our topics of conversation run the gamut. You name it, it's probably been discussed – serious or silly. Some of the serious conversations might be about equipment like, "I'm thinking of getting a different boat," or "I need new oars," and then the pros and cons of various options are discussed. Or, as we get older, a frequent topic is health. "What do you do for the arthritis in your hands," or "Did acupuncture help your sciatica?" with suggestions from personal experience or others' experiences bandied about. On the silly side, you'll often find one of us talking to or about Patita, our little stuffed mascot that Martha typically brings on trips along with Patita's accoutrements – life jacket, jewelry, hat. She even had a little boat at one time! Patita was kidnapped on a Deso trip once. The ransom note was written in letters cut out from a magazine. The ransom was exactly 23 juniper berries or Patita would be hanged from a Cottonwood for the buzzards to eat! Needless to say, we complied with the kidnapper's wishes.

We don't suffer on these trips. Our meals are multi-course gourmet. We start with an appetizer that can range from a fancy charcuterie with a selection of cheeses and meats, to simple chips and guacamole. Main courses are as varied and delicious as the women who make them. Most of our trips have vegetarians, pescatarians and, as my friend Lynne used to say, "meatatarians." We accommodate gluten-free and lactose intolerance. Gals are forced out of their usual menus to come up with some great meals. There's Asian, Mediterranean, and Mexican fare. We eat home-grown basil pesto with lentil noodles, quiche with potato crust, Nat's super salmon or Martha's delicious standby, Mondo Bizzarro (a jazzed-up pesto) among other tempting entrees. Then there are the delicious desserts which we never seem to be too full to pass by. Often, they involve chocolate and are homemade: bars, brownies, and cakes; Zan makes Key Lime Pie on the river, "It's all chemistry, not cooling" she says; or it might be some fancy imported chocolate or simple but mouthwatering Pepperidge Farm cookies. Alcohol is always free flowing. Once camp is set up, cocktail hour starts. "Hour" is a misnomer because it often extends until bedtime. We drink pre-made Margaritas (traditional with only lime, tequila, some form of orange liqueur and ice as the mixer), fancy martini variations, and almost always wine – boxed and of late canned because carrying glass on river trips isn't a good idea. Even after considerable imbibing, we look out for each other. And now almost all of us carry a pee bucket so after we go to bed, we don't have to wander down to the river to relieve ourselves and potentially end up in the drink. (See Martha's Appendix on River Etiquette.)

It seems we have been a positive example for quite a few women over the years. I believe we have inspired others with our ladies' trips. We've run into women getting ready for a mixed trip who have said, "I want to be with you." It's not that they want to ditch their men, but that they'd like to be part of a strong, independent group of women. We have motivated others to think about putting together their own all-female trips. I do hope they were able to follow through. They won't regret it. Don't get me wrong. There is nothing wrong with mixed river trips. They're just different.

I do have a favorite story: We were rigging our boats at the put-in for the Desolation and Gray section of the Green River. The next morning Doreen and I were in charge of the put-in breakfast. This first breakfast on the river can be a challenge because if you're carrying the kitchen and stove, you have to wait until breakfast is over, cleaned up, and everything is packed away before you can finish loading your boat. That evening, as we were hanging out, I said to Doreen "You know, if we don't make coffee in the morning, we won't have to get the stove and kitchen out. That would be easier." I wish I had a camera for the totally shocked expression on Nancy's face! We looked at each other and started laughing. Nancy and the other coffee drinkers not only need but cherish that first cup of camp coffee in the morning. Sitting in your chair, enjoying the company of your companions, and looking at the river in the early morning light as you enjoy that first sip of good strong, coffee is as priceless as the look on Nancy's face. There was coffee the next morning, but after that, Nancy started bringing her own Jetboil so she could whip up a cup regardless. I know she understood where I was coming from, but there was no way she was going to skip morning coffee!

Times like this are what give us the wonderful camaraderie of our ladies' trips. There are the rapids, the floating, the flips, the hikes, the camps, the wind, and weather challenges, and all the beautiful and interesting things that we see and share. But what really stays with me are the treasured friendships I have made on these trips. That's the best part.

Mel carrying her shade on a hike up
Slickhorn on the San Juan River

Even Virtuous Women Want to Tell!
Meeche White

*"What happens on the river stays on the river," is our
version of the famous Vegas saying. In camp on the river,
we can let loose without worrying about the consequences.
Meeche White tells about one wild night with the ladies.*

*It was because of Meeche that ladies' river trips got started
in the first place! She co-founded the National Ability
Center in Park City in 1985 (Adaptive sports, recreation
and adventures – National Ability Center [discovernac.
org]). Its mission is to: "empower individuals of all
abilities by building self-esteem, confidence and lifetime
skills through sport, recreation and educational
programs." All women river trips seemed like a great way
to meet NAC goals, so Meeche contacted the women she
had guided with near Winter Park, Colorado, and, in the
early 90s, a tradition was born. Thank you Meeche. May
the power of ladies' trips continue far into the future!*

I t started quite innocently one evening on the river
when the bread in the Dutch oven was taking
particularly long to bake, and the natives were getting
hungry and impatient. This was in the early 90s, shortly
after our ladies' trips started. The restless women
included a group of friends from work and from my old job
as a rafting guide. To appease them I grabbed a bottle of
citrus vodka designated for another evening. I announced
a new game where one would tell, "If there was anyone in
the world you could 'do,' who would that be?" Upon
naming your hottie, you took a guzzle of vodka and
passed the bottle to the next vixen. This was in the days
of the stunning appeal of Brad Pitt, Matthew
McConaughey, Richard Gere, Denzel Washington, and
some oldies like Clark Gable sprinkled in. Just writing
this makes me want to take a big swig of citrus vodka at
9:00 am on a Sunday morning!

What made this game so intriguing was that women who normally don't drink or drank very little could not wait to get their hands on that bottle – it was a phenomenon! Some women wanted to skip the circle and immediately name yet another potential conquest. The game continued until the bottle was emptied, leaving some of the inexperienced players over-imbibed. One player even ended up sleeping under the kitchen table! We courteously covered her with her sleeping bag – a lesson in moderation.

There were only a few rules to our on-the-river-invented game Swallow and Tell: 1) Wait your turn. 2) You cannot repeat a name. 3) The chef for dinner must serve a somewhat substantial meal to avoid unwanted spewing later in the evening. 4) No camping on a cliff!

Highly recommended for the young at heart!

Meeche hiking near her home in Park City, Utah

Paddlin' Madeline's Limerick
Madeline (Maddie) Dannewitz

Escaping an oppressive religion when she was in her teens, Maddie enrolled herself in whitewater guiding school in northern California. There she rowed the Trinity for several seasons. That's where she met fellow-rafter, Zane, and a romance ensued. Maddie and Zane are now living on the front range of Colorado. In the summer she's a guide with Zane on the Poudre River. When she's not guiding, she studies speech-language pathology and audiology at the University of Northern Colorado.

The sedulous women of the river
Are connected at the soul, sisters
These birds of a feather paddle together
A liquid love that will last forever
Our whitewater worship originates within Her

Maddie in a secluded spot up a side canyon

Coming Into My Own
Shelly Andrews

*Many women are introduced to whitewater through
romances or friendships with men who are whitewater
enthusiasts. Shelly Andrews tells her story of how her
relationship with rivers moved beyond that phase when
she began connecting with river running women.*

*Shelly has been rafting with the ladies for over a decade.
Her first career was with the state of Utah in
environmental quality. She is now a registered nurse with
skills that we, so far, haven't had to take advantage of.
Coupling her early kayaking experience with rafting
makes her a very capable boater. Her calm and easy
countenance are a grace to any river trip. Shelly lives in a
beautiful little town in northern Utah where her first love
is now being a grandmother, passing her love of the
natural world on to the younger generation.*

I learned how to whitewater kayak because I had a
boyfriend who kayaked. Isn't that the way many
women take up an adventure sport? I took a couple of
pool classes from Gary Nichols, the kayaking guru who
was teaching at the University of Utah pool. I learned a
fairly consistent roll. My boyfriend and I kayaked many
rivers together on increasingly difficult whitewater and I
became an adequate class III boater. After a few years,
we started to drift apart, and I found myself without a
companion with whom to paddle down rivers.

I could have stopped boating but that would have made
me a bystander, no longer a part of the moving, living,
flow of the river that I would otherwise have only viewed
from the shore or out of a car window. For me, it was the
most adventurous sport I had ever pursued. It occurred to
me that running rapids far away from civilization
presented some risk. And now, there was no boyfriend to
rescue me after an unexpected mishap. It made every

39

movement feel like it should be undertaken with purpose. I had a heightened awareness that it was up to me to use my own good judgment on the water and then react appropriately. I had to be prepared for a myriad of issues that could come up on a multi-day trip.

I was working for the State of Utah with a woman, Nancy, who was active in river running. Where she went, other boaters went. She invited me on the first of many women's river trips. It was all women, with their own boats and gear and river maps. It changed my life.

Over the years, I've met many strong, independent, and adventurous women who leave their husbands and companions behind to share these unique experiences with other women. A different kind of trust forms between people when they face situations together on the river. It's substantial and lasting, more so than working in a safe office environment or having lunch with a friend in the city. You trust that everyone will come with the needed group gear and there will be enough food to feed the group. It takes skill to make an amazingly fresh Bok choy and pineapple salad on river day six with delicious homemade dressing. After a few years, I bought a raft and discovered the relative comfort and luxury that kayaks don't provide. Now I can bring ice!

Besides the usual deep conversations and plenty of laughter about every topic from relationships, kids, work, and health, we talk about how to load the boat more evenly or how to approach and run a rapid. On the river, I can take the time to listen and really know someone. I can focus on my inner thoughts without checking the phone. At times, it requires my full concentration to maneuver on powerful, rushing, foaming, noisy whitewater. It is a forced meditation that blots out other distractions and thoughts and fills up all my senses. It's a chance to be open to new ideas and skills that are useful both on and off the river. It's the time to overcome fear when your mouth is too dry to make spit. It's freedom from schedules and relaxing into the rhythm of the sun and moon and stars. Boating with these women, I've made lifelong friendships and companions for other kinds of adventures.

Many of the women are what I would describe as secular humanists. Several of us grew up with a religious persuasion but over time have become more freethinking. Morality isn't learned from an ancient book, nor does it find the truth in any one text or philosophy. Yuval Noah Harari writes that when facing a problem, secularists weigh feelings, examine a wide range of observations, possibilities, and information, and cause the least possible harm. That seems to be the women's unspoken river etiquette toward nature and each other. I remember camping above the Middle Fork of the Salmon River at Sunbeam, Idaho, almost forty years ago and watching as a few boaters floated by. I was just a spectator, longing for a connection to something unseen, to wind lazily around the next bend, to be another species existing in nature like our ancient selves.

That's what the women's trips have given me. An opportunity to participate in the natural world. Priceless memories for today and far off tomorrows. Confidence and independence acquired by stepping out of my comfort zone with a little help from my friends. Bring on the next adventure.

Shelly, relaxing next to the river

Virga
Deborah Hughes

Leaving lay the heavy,
Carving pseudonyms in sandstone,
Rain gives up to gravity
In its desire to join with river.

Wearing only sandals,
Carrying only water,
I wander down dry washes
In my desire to join with river.

I am just another veil
The river wears
To woo the rain
Into its bed.

Womentors: The Story of "Rafter V"
Nikki Naiser

*Many women find it difficult to learn whitewater skills
from a well-meaning spouse or romantic partner. Perhaps
it is the pressure of maintaining the dynamics of the
relationship while learning in sometimes-tense situations;
or maybe it is because men and women often have different
learning styles. Nikki Naiser honors her woman rafting
mentor, Velma McMeekin, in this story of how Nikki's
skills developed when Velma took her under her wing.*

She looked like Mrs. Santa Claus: full, rosy cheeks;
bright, hazel eyes; wire-rimmed glasses; silver hair
in a topknot; pleasantly plump in her long dress. I
was sure I had zeroed in on the wrong person. I looked at
my friend, Karen. "Her?" "Yes, that's Velma." Not what I
expected!

I had drawn a San Juan River permit and I was planning
my very first, all-women river trip. I invited Karen to
come along while we were chatting at this way-fun party,
and she told me I *had* to meet Velma. She was a living
legend. She had rowed the Grand twenty plus times, back
when you could do it multiple times in a year. She had
been one of the original Bridger Bowl Ski Area "dirt
bags." She *lived* to float rivers. I expected a svelte, active-
looking type, maybe wearing a little Prana sundress and
Chaco sandals. Not that look, for sure, but she was
beautiful in her way. Indeed, I later learned her
nickname was "Veenie," for Venus, goddess of love. I
heard only teasers about how she came to earn that
moniker back in the day, and so from time to time, my
imagination took over and I created vivid mental
scenarios about her conquests.

Velma came on that ladies' San Juan trip. She was on her
way down to raft with other friends on the Salt River, in

Arizona, so she could only join us for a few days. She took out at Mexican Hat – the only alternate take-out, which was at mile twenty-seven of the eighty-three-mile trip. Velma was so light, so much fun, and she knew what she was doing: the real deal. Her equipment wasn't top-of-the-line, but with her engineer's mind she prepped and rigged in clever, resourceful ways. The few days we were with her she taught us dozens of little tricks by example: how much better one can sleep on a cot; how to handle trash so it takes less room and smells better; how to organize a river kitchen; how to make the *best* river cocktails! We were awed at how efficiently she got ready to launch every morning. She was always the first one ready and used the rest of her time helping us novices get our gear together.

Velma invited me on countless river trips, welcoming me into her river family. When I met her, I had been running whitewater rivers for twenty years. Like many, including Velma, I started paddling whitewater in a tandem canoe back in the eighties. My husband-to-be and I were both learning to paddle and read whitewater at the same time: a recipe for disaster. We lived in Logan, Utah, and cut our whitewater teeth on the beautiful Alpine Canyon section of the Snake River in Wyoming, described as "full of class III action!" We paddled an inherited Royalex Blue Hole OCA, which weighed about eighty pounds – what many back then would call a "divorce boat." The weight of the boat itself made it a struggle for us to hoist onto the roof rack, Rick being six feet tall and me only five feet, four inches. Because most of our early paddling was of the white-knuckle variety, we would often blame each other for whatever went wrong. Rick and I eventually became a competent paddling team, but not without some tumultuous years.

Following job opportunities, we moved to the Seattle area, a river runners' Mecca. I counted 100+ runnable day trips within a two-hour drive from our home. Most of the rivers there were more technical than the pool-drop rivers we

45

had become accustomed to. I was working a big, corporate job, sixty hours a week, and although Rick had a challenging job too, he found more time to boat. He started running the OCA as a solo boat and hooked up with a group of top-notch open canoers. He bought a new Dagger Impulse and was soon doing rolls with that canoe on the open water. Juggling motherhood and corporate demands, I lagged behind on developing river skills; I did take a kayaking class and kayaked with Rick in his open canoe and three other kayaking friends on the class II-III Owyhee River in Idaho. As we independently polished our whitewater skills, we began to trust each other more, and that's when we tightened up our game in the tandem canoe.

When our son, Sam, was three, we decided to fix up a used fourteen-foot Riken raft so we could more easily take Sam along with us. Rick was always the captain, and I took care of Sam, the food, and the kid gear. After we moved to Bozeman, we took the Riken on the Colorado through the Grand Canyon in 1999. It was my first time down there. In our little fourteen-footer with a group of sixteen- and eighteen-footers rowed by mostly twenty-somethings (*we* were in our forties), it was a magnificent adventure. I may have rowed a bit on flat sections, but I barely touched the oars. I went as a passenger on a second Grand trip in 2004. Again, I barely touched the oars, but this time I was dying to gain the confidence to row when our own permit was to come up in 2005 – and I did!

So . . . captaining the Riken on that first San Juan women's trip with Velma in 2004, I had a handle on reading water, but I was just beginning to learn to row. My experience learning with my husband in the boat was not easy: his well-meaning instruction turned into impatience; I became nervous and intimidated; and it *just didn't work*! Velma's way was more like flowing with the river and less like fighting the current.

46

I boated with Velma many times over the next eight years. She was relaxed and clearly appreciated the river and being with her friends on every trip. She was generous with her knowledge and wit, offering suggestions on how to finesse and work with the current. She set an example: a competent woman who had nothing to prove. Velma retired early from her career as one of only a few women working as a technician in the field with AT&T, proving that talent and skill, not gender, gets the job done. She always said her engineering mind came from her father, not from any formal education. She was well-read, inquisitive, and a problem solver.

Velma's boat was precisely outfitted to accommodate her style of rowing and camping, and her rigging was meticulous. Her first time rowing a raft, on the Smith River in Montana, she flipped and lost her friend's dutch oven. She would never let anything like that happen again. It was clear that everything about Velma's way was well thought out: the order in which things were put away; how everything was cleaned out before stowing (no sand in the bottom of that bag!); how the trash was separated and the handwash buckets were stowed last, so you could clean your hands at the end of the process. Most boaters establish habits like these over time, but Velma's ways were more clever and more punctilious than most. And for every quirky process, there was always a good reason why. It all made sense and her efficient methods made trips more enjoyable.

Once she invited me on a trip and my boat wasn't available, so I was Velma's passenger. Like all of us, Velma had her idiosyncrasies, and this experience helped me see a different side of her. Velma loved her boat and liked to have everything just so. She was exceptionally picky about rigging. I considered myself adept, and I knew better than to overstep my bounds on another person's boat. But still . . . at times she seemed over the top. After a couple of days, I became irritated during rigging, loading, and unloading. She trained everyone on how she wanted things on her boat, and when people didn't do it the right way, she let them know. It occurred to me that, annoyed as I was, ninety-five percent of the things Velma did were brilliant. As for the other five percent, it was best to just shut up and do it anyway!

Velma could be no-nonsense, but she was also fun, kind and thoughtful, and she was aware when she crossed the line. Later, after her knees began to fail, Velma was on a rainy Deso/Gray trip, and she was achy and grumpy. Her friends had to do a lot more for her then, choosing camps she could easily access. As the group was putting up the rainfly, she got so upset about something she snapped at all of them. Right away, she and Karen locked eyes and she acknowledged, "I probably shouldn't have said it that way."

Velma learned from friends, books, trial and error, and the river itself, having rowed hundreds of trips. In turn, Velma mentored many: women, men, and children. From the time she was a young child, Bob and Colleen's daughter Cass shadowed Velma, later becoming a river guide and expert kayaker.

Velma died on July 4, 2012, ready to leave the house to meet her sister and friends to float the Yellowstone. When she didn't show up at the meeting spot (before everyone had cell phones), a friend went to check on her and found her motionless on the floor, dressed for the river. In the words of her obituary, "'Rafter V's' generous heart simply could no longer keep pace with her active lifestyle, and it suddenly quit beating on Independence Day."

Velma was larger than life. Her friends and family appreciated her kindness, thoughtfulness, generosity, dedication, integrity, selflessness, compassion – and sheer joy. The way Velma was honored is a testament to the impact she had on so many. Friends contributed to an effort to build a bench and inset a plaque in her honor in a boulder overlooking the Yellowstone River. They produced hats and stickers with the "Rafter V" brand that graced her gear. And they built seven beautiful, miniature dories that carried her ashes down her favorite rivers: the Main Salmon, the Middle Fork of the Salmon, the Green (Deso/Gray), the Colorado (Grand Canyon), the San Juan, the Smith, and the Yellowstone.

Rafter V, Velma, enjoying a jet-boat ride up the Main Salmon River to start a trip at the Corn Creek put-in

Over the years I have learned about rivers and rafting from many women *and* men, and I appreciate them all. But Velma had a greater impact on me than any other. There is something different, something special, about how Velma and my other "womentors" convey their knowledge and skill. Perhaps it comes from a deep understanding of how it feels to be uncertain. Experienced river women seem to exhibit both an inner calm and confidence. They show their strengths in easy, unassuming ways, and they have a willingness to reveal vulnerabilities. After feeling dominated in some of their own experiences, they subtly teach by example rather than by lecture. They are quick to encourage and slow to criticize.

My women boater friends are a kind and generous lot. Just as we all learn, we all teach. On many a river trip, I notice couples in rafts captained by men, with women who are reluctant to get behind the oars. Often the men will strongly encourage – or try to push – their partners to row. I sometimes invite these women passengers onto my boat. Some have said they have a good enough time as passengers, but I have also learned that many have given up: they have recoiled from the way their well-intentioned men try to impart their knowledge and skills.

That's when I strive to embody Velma's way. I gently encourage. I laugh. I teach in a way that is more like flowing with the river and less like fighting the current. So that I, myself, can pass along to other women the joy that is rowing my own boat.

Section Two: Rites of Passage

Growing Up on Desert Rivers
Kelly Robinson

When children are given the freedom to explore wild rivers, they thrive. While many of us have reared our children and grandchildren to appreciate the rivers we love, few of us are of a generation that had river trip opportunities growing up.

Having boated with her family since she was seven, Kelly Robinson shares her memories of being the kid on river trips. She was born in Heidelberg, Germany, and grew up in Salt Lake City, Utah. Kelly is a fourth generation Utahn and shares the adventurous spirit of her mother, Nancy, who introduced her to our ladies' trips. Kelly works in a clinic as a risk manager, which was particularly challenging during the COVID-19 pandemic. Kelly's also raising two boys, so these days she doesn't get on many ladies' trips. When she does, it's a delight to have her younger energy and fresh perspective. An avid mountain biker and skier, Kelly knows how to take advantage of opportunities and suck the marrow out of life! You'll often find Kelly in Southern Utah, enjoying the red rock canyons and, whenever she can, carrying on the family tradition of rafting.

My first river trip was down Desolation and Gray Canyons on the Green when I was seven. It was 1977. I didn't have to comb my hair, shower, or even wear shoes! Not every kid dreams of these freedoms, but I did. I was brought up in Utah where the ideal woman kept a clean home and raised a nice family. But there are also Utah women who run rivers in the summer and ski in the winter, women who don't mind whether water is filtered and prefer sleeping under the stars.

I'm not sure why we didn't bring drinking water on that Desolation trip. My mom says it's because it would've taken up too much beer space. Desert rivers are mostly mud. It seemed like it would be impossible to drink, but I'm alive to tell you that river water can be digestible if you let it settle overnight and add Kool Aid. I won't say it tastes good. But for this trip it was the only option – other than beer. I guess tents took up beer space too, because we didn't have tents. I woke up the first morning on the beach with a furry tarantula by my side. Not every kid decides they can live with tarantulas, but I did. I came to realize that sleeping out is magic and tarantulas don't want to hurt you.

When we launched from Sand Wash, we floated away from civilization, and we rarely saw another soul. After four days we ran into a hermit in the middle of nowhere! Back in the seventies, he lived near the clear, running water at Rock Creek with his donkey. We filled our water bottles there, avoiding the need to settle water that night. I spent one of the happiest days of my life playing in the creek and climbing the cottonwoods.

Seven-year-old Kelly climbing a cottonwood

The isolation of these river trips shaped me as a person, and the people I met shaped my world. Mary was a guide on my first trip, the first of many river goddesses I met. She was beautiful with olive skin and exotic features. She taught me to belly dance, and I did gymnastics for her on the beach. My Uncle Dave, a river guide and owner of Harris Boat Trips, told scary stories "to fortify a kid's character," he said. The stories didn't sugarcoat experience; they got you ready to face what the world could throw at you. As we sat around the fire, Dave told us about a Girl Scout leader named Maggie Skagpie, who became horribly disfigured cooking over a campfire when hot oil splashed on her face. In a hushed tone, so Maggie couldn't hear, Dave told us Maggie haunted camps at the bottom of the canyon. He warned us to be sure to secure our gear because Maggie survived by robbing boaters' camps at night. These were the moments that shaped my character – I could be scared, or I could learn to check my gear and be a river runner.

As I tasted the freedom that river trips offer, especially ladies' trips, I began to recognize what the real challenges are. They are not tarantulas or Maggie Skagpies. The challenges are in our culture and institutions. The people who tell you, "Girls can't wear baseball hats and shouldn't hold frogs." Out in the wilderness you figure out what's real. To survive, you have to learn who you are and what you're made of.

It's a rare year when all the smaller desert rivers flow. About every decade there's enough water to run canyons that you can usually only hike – the Muddy, the San Rafael, and the Price. In my twenties I ran these three rivers in three days. It was around 1990. We did a river a day, camped at the end, and headed to the next river the next day. In 2019, when I was forty-nine, it was another rare water year. My kids had fledged, and I was between jobs. The river goddesses favored me. If I was going to be fired, that was a good year. I may not have fit into some places in Utah, but I was born to adventurous Utahns who showed me how to navigate its wild places. Hell, I didn't have a job so why not head to the desert my family had introduced me to?

I didn't run the three rivers consecutively in 2019 like I did in 1990. I skipped the Price and started with the Muddy. It was much tougher than I remembered. But running it, I felt free and strong. When you see the log jam high above you at the narrowest part of the canyon, you realize that it doesn't get any more remote or more beautiful than this. What a feeling to touch the walls as you slide through!

Log jam twenty feet above the water line on Muddy Creek

I moved on to my favorite river, the San Rafael. By 2019, the crowds had found this river. It has everything – incredible geology, intriguing archaeology with petroglyphs and pictographs, a uranium mine, a spring, red rock walls, swallows circling high above, and rock wrens singing down a minor scale. Then I ran the Dolores. Its tall salmon walls rivaled anything I'd seen before. There were bighorn sheep, good camps, fun rapids, and the store where the movie *Thelma & Louise* (a 1991 American film centered around two female friends and their road-crime drama) was filmed. Somehow, I felt a connection to those two rebels.

How do you get to places like the Muddy? You can't depend on your GPS. The directions head you into nowhere, then the road splits into a crossroad and you have to decide which is the right one and hope for the best. If you made the right choice, you dead-end at an old mine where you either risk the steep rocky drive down to the takeout, or if you don't drive down, you hump all your stuff down the hill. But there you are! You found it.

I've been on Idaho rivers and kayaked in Alaska. I've floated Washington rivers and lived and recreated on the Gulf Coast. But there's something different about the Utah desert rivers. They give me what I need. They're impossible. They're magical. They're real. These rivers are for girls who don't mind getting dirty. Girls who must sleep out to recharge. They're also for belly dancers and young gymnasts. They're for cowgirls who love cowboys, and women who would rather have a river rock than a diamond. They're the place I go when I need to connect to myself . . . when I need to be recharged by women who love the same desert rivers that I do.

Kelly loving a desert river somewhere

Rites of Passage

Lauri Kloepfer

The role of rivers in our lives shifts as we grow through life's changes. Rivers teach us to rely on ourselves. They offer respite from the challenges of working motherhood. Later, we proudly look on as we pass the torch to our own daughters, as they become competent river women themselves.

Lauri Kloepfer recounts the significance of rivers as she navigates her life. Lauri grew up on a lake in South Dakota sailing, canoeing, and water skiing. As a young woman she taught canoeing at a YWCA camp for four years. Lauri took her first raft trip while going to college in Bozeman, Montana. When she transferred to Utah State University in Logan, Utah, she learned to kayak and raft. For several years Lauri worked as a river guide on the Main Salmon River in Idaho. After she became an educator, her summers were filled with river trips with friends and family. She married Jack Kloepfer in 1985 after fishing him out of an eddy in his kayak. After so many years on the river, she and Jack are now playing in the ocean in Mexico with their paddleboards. From the lake to the river and now the ocean, water has always been a part of Lauri's life.

Being on the river comes down to one thing for me: rites of passage. Boating is freedom, friendships, and depending on yourself. Freedom is floating down the river enjoying the sound of the water and the beauty of your surroundings as you slip deeper into a canyon. Friendships and teamwork are a part of all trips. Everyone pitches in and helps, and we all watch out for each other. But the moment you are on the river in your kayak with your hands on the paddle or seated in your raft with your hands on the oars, you have to depend on yourself – no one else. Not your boyfriend to put your kayak on his rack, not your husband to make a boat for you, but yourself. I am not saying that it isn't wonderful to go on trips with other people, or that there's not an inter-dependency on river trips, but when you are a foot away from a huge hole, it is about you. When your kayak is upside down, it is about you. Boating with women has helped me grow as a person and taught me these things.

My first river rite of passage was when I was kayaking. I lived in Logan, Utah, and we used to go over the state line to the Bear River in Idaho. We'd wait for the water to come up with the daily release of irrigation water from the dam and jump in our kayaks to go down the river. One day my boyfriend wanted to go boating after work. I was teaching at the time and after my students left, I tore home, changed clothes, and went to get my boat. He had left without me, and I didn't have a rack for my kayak. !@*#$! The next week I bought an Olympic Quick N Easy Rack and put it on my vehicle.

I resolved to never again depend on my boyfriend, or anyone else for that matter, to get me to the river. I still had fun tandem whitewater canoeing. But in a kayak, I didn't need a partner to get down the river and I could float whenever I wanted to.

The next rite of passage was my first ladies' trip. Sometime in the early 90s, my friend Karen said, "Let's go on a ladies' trip." "Sure." We went down the San Juan with a bunch of women boaters from the Glenwood Springs area. What a blast! We pampered ourselves on spa days, played drinking games, went on spectacular hikes, and made lasting friendships. Ladies' trips have a special energy. Power and determination are laced with friendship and care. Peeing in the river in front of the girls is easier than when there are men around, and we never forget to put a pee bucket by the groover. Underwear is optional, which really makes peeing easy!

My early ladies' trips evolved into recovering mother trips. I had many boating girlfriends with young children. We were on the go and in a general state of exhaustion all the time. When we could, three to five of us would hop in Fat Cats, kayaks, or canoes and go on the San Juan or the Dolores. Our goal on these trips was rest, not work, so we made everything as simple as possible. We'd set up camp in five minutes or less with one big, shared tent. We'd pull the groover off the boat and put it up right there next to the river instead of traipsing around looking for the perfect groover spot. We used a backpacker stove and kept meals easy. Dinner was usually ramen noodles or burritos, both paired with tequila. Best of all we sleep-deprived moms SLEPT for ten hours every night. Ahhhhh. After taking care of ourselves for several days we could go back and take care of everyone else. Going on these ladies' trips was much more helpful than any parenting book I ever read.

Introducing my girlfriends, nieces, and my daughter to river trips was another rite of passage. The list is long: My goddaughter, Annie, came out for years to go on Desolation with us when she was little. My niece Jill's first river trip was a ladies' trip on the San Juan. She later became a guide. My sister came from South Dakota for her one and only river trip on the Yampa. It was a wonderful trip full of music and laughter. Morgan, another niece, joined me on Gates of Lodore when she was seventeen. Karen and I did so many trips together that we only needed one-word phone conversations to plan a trip, "Roll-a-Table?" "Yes." Back then we could get ready for most week-long river trips in two hours, and a three-week Grand trip in a day! My best friend from high school and college roommate came with me on a San Juan Trip *and* a Grand Canyon Trip. I still have a great video of her doing a back flip off the paddle boat in the middle of a series of rapids called the Roaring Twenties. Another college roommate and I reunited on a girls' trip after boating separately in different states for years. I boated frequently with my sister-in-law, Nancy. I married her brother, Jack, after he took me on my first Grand Canyon trip.

There's a special bond that happens on the river that I haven't experienced anywhere else. It is the perfect place to strengthen existing love and friendships. Most of my friends are river friends, and I'm so happy I share that bond with my family.

One of my favorite rites of passage happened with my daughter. There were four lady boating friends in Durango, and we all had daughters the same age. They all learned to kayak and row rafts. When our daughters were eighteen, we went on a San Juan ladies' trip, and they all rowed or kayaked. We took mud baths and drank tequila. We passed the torch to the next generation on that trip, and the following year my daughter rowed her dad down the Grand Canyon! Three of the four girls became river guides, including one who guides on the Grand Canyon *and* the Middle Fork of the Salmon – the two rivers considered to be the toughest in the West.

Lauri rowing down Deso with 18-month-old daughter, Kate,
in a Paco Pad play pen

Thinking back, these river trips all seem to blend together
– trips with family, trips with friends, trips with the girls.
My memories are a jumble. They float by like a mirage:
laughing together, the rhythm of rigging, tents flying into
the river, hunkering down in a monsoon or snow storm,
trying to get out of the sun, floating on Paco Pads, driving
to a put-in, fixing flats, snacking on the boat, singing in
the morning, rolling in the mud, enjoying happy hour,
cooking dinner, taking hikes, seeing scorpions and
snakes, and sharing everything from toothbrushes to
laughter and, of course, love. What a wonderful time I've
had. I'm forever grateful for my river family and friends .
. . and for the women who have shared my rites of
passage and helped me grow.

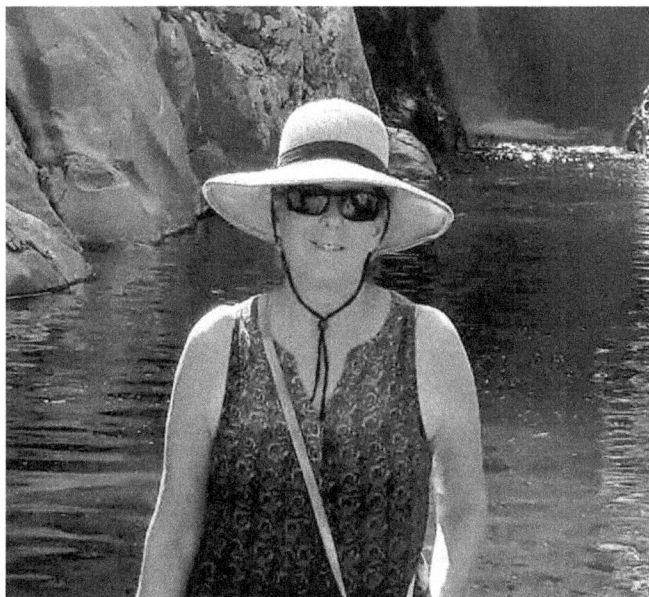

Lauri on the Usumacinta River in southern Mexico

Socks

As told by Teri and Sara Painter to Zan Merrill

*Coming of age can be awkward for all of us. Girls new to
nature's sudden pronouncement of womanhood don't
always think to prepare themselves with the supplies
required to support the changes in our bodies. Teri and
Sara Painter recall such a time on the river with the very
best of company for such an event.*

*Teri found her way out West after growing up north of
New York City and traveling the world. A degree in
Special Education led her to volunteering with Common
Ground in Logan, Utah, an organization that offers river
trips and other outdoor recreation opportunities to people
with disabilities. Sara started coming along on river trips
when she was a little girl. Mother and daughter now live
in different states on opposite sides of the Rockies but they
have their own rafts. Teri and Sara get on the river
whenever they can.*

I was always grateful that Sara was such an easy-going
child. She'd go with the flow, taking things in stride
and seldom getting anxious or upset. Maybe that's
why river running came so naturally to her.

It was our second day on a week-long Desolation River
trip when Sara came up to me as I was rigging our boat
and said, "My period just started. I forgot to bring
anything for it." It wasn't her first period, but it was
among her first. Sara's young body had not yet fallen into
a predictable rhythm of waxing and waning with the
moon. She had made more of a statement than a plea.
Still, we had to figure something out. The solution came
almost instantly. "How many pairs of socks did you
bring?" I asked. "Only two," Sara replied. "Go ask people
if they can give you their spare socks. I have a couple of
big safety pins in my first aid kit. We can pin the socks to

your panties, then you can rinse them in the river, stick them in a baggie, and rinse them in clear water when you get to camp. Here, I have a couple of baggies with my lunch stuff." Sara didn't ponder long, "That's a great idea, Mom. What do I say if people want to know what the socks are for?" "Just ask the women. Tell them what's going on if they ask. They'll get it. They'll be happy to help. Oh, and maybe it's a good idea now that you're getting your periods to always bring some Tampons on these trips." Sara nodded and off she went.

By evening all the women had gotten wind of what was going on. We hiked a little ways up Cedar Ridge Canyon, where we improvised a short ceremony welcoming Sara to womanhood. One of the gals gave a lovely speech, another presented Sara with a heart-shaped rock she'd found on the beach, and one collected a little bouquet of flowers. We all basked in the sweetness of the moment, recalling our own journeys. Sara smiled as knowing glances flitted between the older women.

Teri and Sara enjoying each other's company on Labyrinth

Confluence
Deborah Hughes

2,000 feet down
Two rivers meet.

The Green offers up
Its current to the Colorado,

Their headwaters distant
And in differing states,

Yet join here
In these depths

For a dance
Through the Grand,

To empty
With all the others flowing,

To begin again as rain.

There's Been an Accident
Zan Merrill

*As we float wild rivers, life in the outside world goes on –
or ends, in some cases. Zan Merrill tells the story of a river
trip none of us will ever forget, and the group of women
who were there for her during a shocking and devastating
time of loss.*

*Zan came late to rafting – she was almost fifty – and she
came even later to this group of women rafters. Although
she fell in love with the river on her first trip down the
Grand Canyon in her late twenties, she didn't see guiding
as a path for her. Instead, she earned a couple of degrees
and launched an interesting career in training design.
Twenty years later, after a second Grand trip, she realized
it was now or never if she wanted to get into rafting. She
bought a boat with a couple of girlfriends and that was
that. Now Zan has her own boats and gets on the river
every chance she gets. She also enjoys doing textile art,
writing, hiking, birding, and yoga.*

About the time Peter was distracted by a Peregrine
falcon as he drove along the red sandstone cliffs in
Colorado National Monument, missed a turn, and
plummeted 150 feet, I reckon I was looking at Desecration
Panel on the San Juan River. Peter lived long enough for
the ranger and medics to find him. I'm glad someone was
with him when he died. While I wish I had been with him,
if I had, I probably would have died, too. Peter was my
partner of almost forty years. He was a remarkable man.
You knew when Peter walked into a room. I didn't learn
of the accident until a couple of days after it happened. I
wouldn't have learned about it for over a week if it hadn't
been for my brothers, the San Juan County sheriff, and
our selfless shuttle driver Jim Hardin.

Peter Küng on a Desolation trip a few years before his death

Three days before the crash a bunch of gals from around the West – eleven of us –met late in the afternoon just outside of Bluff, Utah, at the launch for the San Juan River. There were a few from Durango, one from near Winter Park, and me from the West Slope of Colorado, five women came from northern Utah, and one from Bozeman, Montana. It was a few days past the summer solstice, and it was hot – over 100. We waited until the evening cooled things off a bit before we rigged, then drove to the other end of Bluff for dinner at the Twin Rocks Café. Good grub and it was simpler than breaking out, cleaning up, then repacking our camp kitchen.

We launched the next morning. My friend, Penny, had pulled the permit. She has a fifteen-foot, self-bailing Maravia and didn't want to row alone. So, I left my little twelve-foot cataraft at home, and we partnered up. It's always a joy to be on the river with Pen. She's an excellent oars woman, a fisheries biologist who knows a lot of interesting facts, and she's fun. We laugh a lot when we're together. I looked forward to spending some one-on-one time with her, catching up with my other river buddies, and getting to know a couple of gals from Durango I hadn't met.

Our first day on the river dawned early and warm, and the river was running high and fast. Before we knew it, we'd made the hard right turn in the river past Tiger Wall, with its beautiful dark streaks of desert varnish on the salmon sandstone. We slipped past Chinle, where we usually got a permit to hike but not this time, and pulled in at Desecration Panel. The petroglyphs on this panel were created by the Anasazi or Ancient Ones hundreds of years ago. Looking at these petroglyphs is like going through a museum. Instead of walking along walls displayed with artwork, you wander along the base of a 150-200-foot cliff for a quarter mile looking at an artistic, skillful scattering of images. One story of the panel goes that during the flu epidemic of 1918, a Navajo elder had a vision that the bad spirits killing his people emanated from this petroglyph panel. Another story is of a similar vein but happens later in the 20th century. At any rate, in the elder's vision, he was to destroy the petroglyphs, but not all of them. There were specific images where the bad spirits were emerging. He visited the panel with a hatchet and went after the offending petroglyphs, desecrating them by hacking at the stone outlines. But he didn't completely obliterate the figures. He didn't cut out chunks of rock or scrape the 'glyphs off the wall. Instead, with each strike of the hatchet, he meticulously cut oblique angles into the petroglyphs. Did breaking up the lines break the portal for the evil spirits? Who knows, but to my eye his hatches made the sheep look woolly and the human figures look like they were wearing winter gear. As I was looking at the figures where the evil spirits had been vanquished, Peter's spirit – his energy – was rising into the high Colorado desert.

One of the "desecrated" petroglyphs

It was still early in the day after we viewed the panel and then enjoyed lunch in the shade of some cottonwoods. With the river running as fast as it was, we decided to try for Ledges camp. It was another eight and a half miles downriver, but at this level we'd be there in a little over an hour. Ledges is a popular camp. If it was available, we were hoping to spend two nights there and take a layover. It's always nice to take a break from the daily routine of packing up in the morning and setting up camp every day. A layover would give us two nights at the same camp, saving us a little work.

Ledges *was* open. The camp is on river left just after a Class II+ rapid with the same name. Immediately after running the rapid, you must pull hard out of the current to the left to catch a nice eddy in front of camp. There are several ledge levels to pitch tents, throw down a tarp and bag, or set up a cot. The view across the river to the short steep cliff that frames the rapid is pleasant, or you can set up a lower camp to watch the river as it flows down the canyon. The eddy makes for good swimming and lounging in the shallows, which is exactly what we did for our day off when we weren't searching out scant shade from the willows to quell the heat. By the end of the afternoon, we were wondering why we had decided to spend a day in that heat, but I'm glad we did. Otherwise, I wouldn't have found out about Peter's death for another five, maybe six days.

The temperature started to slip into the nineties, not much of a cool-down, but it felt better. Cocktail hour was finished and so was a satisfying, communal dinner. We were sitting in our camp chairs chatting and sipping wine when we noticed a lone hiker coming up the opposite bank along the crest of the cliff. It was dusk – late for someone to be hiking. He seemed determined, head down, watching his feet, walking quickly. Usually out in the wilds, folks acknowledge each other. As much as we crave solitude and having the river to ourselves, we *are* sociable and enjoy a wave or quick conversation with people in passing. But this man didn't look up. Our waves in his direction went unanswered. I didn't recognize him as my brother, and I was curious why this man was hiking upriver at this time of day, away from civilization, with only a day pack. I wandered up the beach to watch him a little longer. He stopped fifty yards upstream when he reached river's edge. He was taking his clothes off. I figured he needed to take a quick dip to cool off before going wherever he was going so I turned to give him some privacy and headed back to the girls. I'd settled back into my chair and picked up on the conversation when, "HELP!!! HELP!!!" The hiker had been swept into the rapid. I ran to the last boat in line and started untying

71

the bow line, when I realized that he was rescuing himself. It took a few tries, but he was able to grab a rock and pull himself out of the rapid onto the cliff face. I watched as, quite efficiently, he climbed up the wall. I retied the boat and sat on my haunches next to the river, waiting to see what would happen next. I still didn't recognize Lance. When he got to the top of the cliff he turned and called my name, "Zan! Zan, sit down." He'd taken his glasses off for the swim and mistook Lauri, who stood up for a better view, for me. That's when I recognized him. "I AM sitting down. What are you doing here, Lance?" "Zan, there's been an accident. . . Peter's dead." "WHAT?!" And he repeated, "Peter's dead." I slipped into stunned silence. The other women reacted with shock and confusion.

Still, with daylight fading I knew we needed to get Lance to our side of the river as quickly as possible. I said so and was ready to strip down someone's boat, row across, and rescue my brother. Lauri's a stronger rower than I am and recognized I wasn't quite with it. Still, I wanted to help . . . I needed to help. I needed to be doing something. We unloaded one of the small, more maneuverable catarafts. The plan was for Lauri to row up the eddy and into the rapid, then swing around to face the cliff. As we approached Lance, I'd throw him a line and a life preserver, then we'd get him onto the boat or to shore, whichever scenario worked out. As we were launching, Penny asked if there was anything else we needed. In her short dress, Lauri grinned and said maybe she should have put some underwear on. We all laughed, and Lauri shoved off. She got across the eddy easily and into the rapid. She spun the boat to face the cliff. I shouted instructions, "Jump into the river ahead of us. I'll throw you a line." "NO! Lance shouted, I'll jump in front of the boat and grab it." There was no time to argue. Lance is an old ski jumper with a great sense of timing. His jump into the river was perfect and before I could raise a hand to help him, he'd positioned himself to grab the frame and vaulted onto the raft. He held me in a wet embrace. "Zan, I'm so sorry. I wanted to be the one to tell you, not some stranger. I'm so sorry."

It took Lauri a little more work to ferry the three of us across the river and then back upstream to camp, but her perfect forty-five-degree angle did the trick. We clambered off the raft and into camp.

The light was fading, and Lance and I needed a boat to get down to the four-wheel drive road that goes along the river north of Mexican Hat, where my other brother Chris was waiting in Lance's pickup. First we needed to get across the river so Lance could pick up his pack and the rest of his clothes that he'd left upstream. We decided that the best boat would be Barbara's. She could pair up with Penny since they were both going back to Logan. Penny's boat was big enough to carry all our gear – mine, Barbara's, and Penny's. The girls would break my camp down in the morning.

I felt confused, but through a haze of indecision I grabbed a change of clothes, water bottle, and my overnight stuff and threw them into a small dry bag, while Barbara got the gear off her little cataraft. I filled my bottle, and someone gave us an extra one. After heartfelt good-byes, and more hugs and love from these strong supportive women (and a few chastisements telling Lance to wear a PFD next time he jumped into a river), Lance and I lined the almost empty boat upstream around the point that framed the camp's eddy, then up the bank until we were able to float down to where he had left his things.

I remember it was hard – harder than it should have been – to row across the river. I was breathing heavily when we hit the other shore. Lance jumped off. In the dim light it took a few minutes for him to find his things. I took a long slug of water off my bottle while he was searching.

When Lance was back on board I swung the stern into the current and started rowing. Lance was facing me, looking downstream. I asked him to keep me pointed in the right direction so I could keep facing upstream, the most powerful rowing position. It was getting dark fast, and we had a couple of miles to go. Floating that distance would normally take thirty minutes or so. I didn't relish rowing in the dark. I kept pulling hard.

Lance told me what he knew about the accident: Peter had driven off a cliff in the Monument and died sometime in the afternoon two days ago. The medics and ranger got to Peter just before he passed. Lance didn't know any more details. He said it had been a challenge finding me, but that story was too complicated for right now. "Let's just get our asses out of here. I'll tell you the rest when we get to the motel." "Okay," I said as I started on my second water bottle. "Damn! Why am I so thirsty?" "Shock," was all he had to say. We continued in silence except for the sound of the oars dipping in and out of the water, and the occasional words from Lance to correct our direction. Then he said, "We should be getting close. Chris and I drove as far as we could on that dirt road. I'm sure glad we brought my pick-up and not Chris's car. We got stuck in the sand at one point . . .. There's the camp! Pull in."

Where the road ended there was a river camp. The folks there knew what was going on and helped us as we got to shore. I gave my other brother, Chris, a big hug, and before we knew it, the boat had been loaded and secured onto the back of the pickup. We hit the dirt road – not more than a two-track – just as darkness closed in on the river. On high beams we dodged the ruts out to US-191 and took a left into Mexican Hat, where Lance and Chris had rented a room at the San Juan Inn. We didn't sleep much that night. The trip back to Junction the next day was intense; arranging via cell phone for a mortuary so

Peter's body could be released from the Mesa County Sheriff; listening to the details of how my neighbors found Lance, then how he figured out where I was. He described the crazy drive down to the river in record time, with the help from the San Juan County Sheriff, our shuttle driver, and the BLM. It's all a blur now. In fact, the entire next year was a blur. I never would have made it without the help of my brothers. I never would have made it without my friends, especially my river friends. More than one gal came to spend time with me.

Life goes on. The river goes on. Our river friendships grow stronger as we realize how rare and extraordinary our shared experiences have been. We are strong and capable. We are supportive and accepting. We are fun and a little crazy. We are a bunch of old ladies loving every minute we have, especially when we're on a river.

My heartfelt thanks to the women who shared that fateful trip with me, especially Penny, Lauri, Nancy, Nikki, Mel, Ellen, Barbara, and Kelly.

Zan always with her visor and water bottle across her shoulder

Recovery
Kelly Robinson

*For working women with young children, life can feel
impossible at times. For Kelly Robinson, getting back on
the river presented a plethora of obstacles. Once afloat, she
found a different kind of challenge. Supported by her
strong boatwomen companions, she learned to listen to her
inner voice and found healing in their gentle acceptance.*

At forty years old, I decided to recover from a decade
of the American dream. Keeping a house and
growing two humans – all while working full-time –
drained me. I felt drained of milk, breath, money, and
energy. I emerged from my thirties thirty pounds larger.
At this stage of life, going on a trip – any trip – requires
overcoming a mountain of logistics: finding someone to
drive the kids, cook, help with homework, watch the dogs,
keep an eye on the house, take care of the kids . . .. Forget
cleaning. You know you will return to a wreck. And all
that doesn't even include planning for the trip itself! I was
invited on a women's river trip, which is kind of an honor.
To be honest I was on the brink of a nervous breakdown,
so with support from my mom I put my energy into
making it happen.

It all came together. That first morning I lifted my head
up to see the sandstone cliffs, clouds, and the birds
circling. How long have I had my head down? The mission
of a woman's trip is to get back to yourself. I knew I was
the weakest link on the trip – the youngest and the
farthest removed from myself – but I also knew I was
with a group of understanding, supportive women. My
dad says on a woman's trip, you have to fight the women
to do any work because they are all so helpful. You turn
around and someone has made the fire, set up the

kitchen, and you probably already have a drink in your hand. It was exactly the situation I needed.

Often on mixed trips there is that guy who has to be first. He picks camps, he gets his aerobic work-out, he's in charge. It's usually someone with a little extra testosterone. On women's trips there *are* boaters in the lead, but they are usually simply in such good shape that slowing down is hard. They enjoy the rhythm of rowing, being the first to flush birds from the shore, or floating quietly and enjoying the solitude, sounds and feel of the river. Then someone else in the group catches up and takes the lead.

On one ladies' trip I was the leader . . . of the "slacker group." I adopted the motto, "I do what I want." One of the gals was in really good shape. It was 105 degrees, and the group was headed out for a ten-mile jog to the confluence of the Green and Colorado. I was about ready to join them when I looked around and Janet was settling into her chair with a cold beer. "What!?" I thought, "How can she do that? Everyone is going on the run." She didn't apologize or question her decision. She placed her chair in the water next to the bank and opened a beer. "Hell yeah!" I almost said out loud, "It's just as much of a bad-ass move to sit in the water and do what you want as it is to run ten miles!" I joined her. Janet and I formed the slacker group. I had to ask myself a few times what it *was* I wanted, but when I found my voice, I realized I was in charge of my own energy.

Fast forward twenty years. On this women's trip, would I be considered a slacker? I knew I was out of shape; I was carrying that extra weight I'd gained over the last decade. Coming from oxygen-rich sea level in Florida to over 4,000 feet wouldn't help the situation. Even though most of these women were retired or close to it, they had logged hundreds of hours on the river and were fit and trim. But this was the San Juan River. What could happen on the San Juan? It's warm so there's no possibility of hypothermia. It's relatively flat with only one rapid you need to scout. I was used to the Florida humidity, so this dry heat was pleasant. As long as I drank plenty of water there would be no heat stroke. What could happen? I knew better. I have not been on a trip where there wasn't an incident of some sort. On this trip, a hundred-year flash flood happened. The water rose four feet in a matter of a few hours.

It was in the morning, and we had just launched. I was paddling my Fat Cat, following Karen in her row rig. As she powered into shore so we could stop for a hike, I, unfortunately, couldn't reach the tiny beach sandwiched between Russian olive trees. My boat swept into the thorny bushes, and I flipped. The drawstring on my cool straw hat wrapped around my neck, and I struggled to free myself and not drown as my boat rushed down the river. The rest is legend. Zan saved my fat ass. I was watching my boat fly down the river just out of reach. Janet was in her boat calming me. Zan flung her throw rope to Janet and said, "Hold my boat!" Then she jumped from her boat to my boat, stood on one pontoon, grabbed the straps on the other end, and flipped my boat over. What the hell just happened?!? There were trees flying down this river and this bitch jumps onto my boat, flips it upright and paddles to safety! Are you kidding me? I got on Zan's boat and rowed it in, then sat on the shore shaking from shock. Zan said to me, "We were going into that canyon. I had to do something."

Recovery takes many forms. Helping a young mom get a needed rest is recovery. Teaching a woman to listen to her inner voice and do what feels right is recovery. Being plucked out of the river and getting to shore safely is recovery. The river has always been there for me, my teacher and my healer.

78

A Healing Journey
Michelle Hutchins

*The flow of the river is a metaphor of life. Michelle
Hutchins helps us understand that fighting the current is
not the most effective strategy.*

*Michelle is a Colorado native and a true mountain
woman. Born and raised in Grand County, at an elevation
of 9,000 feet, she has lived there all her life. She taught
skiing for many years at Winter Park Resort. Michelle
enjoys anything the outdoors has to offer, from the Rocky
Mountains to the southwest desert. She is also mom to
three children, all of whom ventured off to other places.
Michelle loves hiking, boating, and traveling in the family
RV. She has entertained us with Tarot cards on ladies'
river trips. Michelle has now taken her adventures to other
places.*

All my suffering is to teach me
I have nothing to fear
Let go of control
Let God be the captain.

Follow the current
Don't fight the flow
I am caught in an eddy
around and around I go.

Soon the weather will change
The water will rise
It will be time to go
I'll be stuck no more.

I will see the view
just beyond the bend
My life course will move forward
I'll soon be free.

In the meantime,
Rest
In the quiet circular motion
and enjoy the reprieve.

Michelle checking out a rock art panel

Section Three: Adventures

Byers Canyon
Martha Hut and Karen Carver

The notorious high-water years of the early eighties offered unprecedented opportunities for whitewater enthusiasts. Martha Hut and Karen Carver recall a crazy run that presented more challenges than they anticipated.

During the high-water years of the early eighties, Karen and I were working for a small rafting company out of Winter Park, Colorado. We ran daily paddle trips on the upper Colorado. Every day on our drive back to Winter Park, we would look at the huge rapid in Byers Canyon and wonder, "Could we run it?" We decided to give it a shot.

Byers Canyon is a steep canyon downstream from the town of Hot Sulfur Springs. The highway runs along one side, and the railroad runs on the other. From both sides, big, sharp rocks have been pushed into the river to keep the highway and the railroad clear. The rocks forming the rapids are jagged, not like the smooth ones worn over time that are normally found in a river.

A few other folks decided to come along and run the rapid that day, including a safety kayaker. We stopped and scouted from the highway, planned our route, and drove upstream to a calm stretch where we could put our boats in the water. This was before the age of helmets and technical splash gear, and we only had wool sweaters and ponchos to wear in the icy water. About forty-five minutes elapsed between the time we scouted and the time we entered the water. We were unaware that a large volume of water had been released at the upstream dam, ready to barrel down on us.

I was rowing a thin-skinned Udisco with Meeche and Bonnie as my crew. They were ready to bail and high side if needed. Just as we entered the rapid, I saw an oar from the boat in front of us fly straight up into the air. I screamed "Oh, no, they flipped." Meeche and Bonnie had a little better vantage and screamed "Yeah, they're over!"

The raft in front of Martha flips in Byers Canyon

It didn't make any difference. There was no turning back. I was running this rapid! When you run an intimidating rapid like Byers, you go into a quiet zone. Your skills and training take over. I was focused, pulling on the oars for all I was worth and keeping the raft straight as we entered the hole. But it wasn't enough. We slammed into a sharp rock at the bottom of the rapid and tore a big hole in the bottom of the boat. I yelled "Bail! Bail!" My crew yelled back "We can't! We have a self-bailer now!" as they clung to the tubes of the boat. Luckily, we made it through without turning over. Joy wasn't so lucky. She had fallen out of the other boat and managed to grab onto a rock. We picked her up as we floated by. She was quite badly battered by all the rocks, but said she'd be alright. When we could, we pulled over to river left – the highway side of the river – where some onlookers helped us pull the boat up the fifty-foot embankment to the road. That's when it sunk in: We'd made it! I had rowed Byers Canyon! As far as I know I was the first female to get through those rocky, rip-rap rapids!

Martha making the move into the big rapid

But our adventure wasn't over. We'd lost the kayak. We drove along the river, stopping at every ranch road and bridge to look for it. We would dash out of the car leaving the doors open, have a quick look, and climb back in, repeating the process at the next vantage point. At one stop, we returned to the van to find a rancher's heeler dog in the front seat. It had claimed the van as its turf and was growling at us. I grabbed a paddle and dangled a piece of lunch meat off the end. "Looky, looky, looky," I cajoled as I held the treat under its nose toward its snarling lips. The dog jumped out after the treat and we jumped in, slammed the doors, and peeled out. We finally found the kayak way downstream.

Our initial plan was to make two runs to give Karen a chance to row and a couple of others to ride through as passengers. We thought better of it. At least for *that* trip!

Martha and Karen hiking a side canyon on the
Rio Chama, New Mexico

My River Adventures

Nancy Hess

*We all come to the river from different directions, and we
all have different journeys once we're hooked. Nancy Hess
tells about her early trips, and how she earned the
moniker "Low-Water Nancy."*

*Nancy has been rowing since she was a young woman,
and nothing frazzles her. She introduced us to smaller,
single person catarafts made by her younger brother, and
she always has an extra boat to loan. Now retired, Nancy
managed to get lots of river trips in even when she was
working for the State of Utah. She continues to work in a
few trips every year sandwiched between traveling,
enjoying time with her grand kids, and spending winters
in Mexico. Nancy gently, but consistently reminds us OCD
types that there's more to rafting than packing up early
and getting a good workout as we row from point A to B.
With all her associations on the river, she's as close as we
get to river royalty.*

My western river adventures began in 1973 on a
Grand Canyon trip with my brother David's river
company, Harris Boat Trips. Dave was a young
man looking to change his life direction. To get things
rolling he hung around Lees Ferry, where Grand Canyon
rafting trips start, hoping to get on a trip. He'd help load
boats and run odd errands until finally, one of the
outfitters invited him to go down the river as a swamper,
a "general assistant" of sorts. Duties included what Dave
was already doing – loading boats – but on the river he
was also unloading, helping set up camp, assisting in the
kitchen, helping clients, and doing whatever the guides
asked of him. Dave was competent, ambitious, and a
quick learner. In a short time, after successful runs
through easier rapids and a couple of closely scrutinized
tougher rapids, he was running the big, motorized boats

on his own. Soon his girlfriend, Linda, joined him, and within a couple of years they owned Harris Boat Trips.

Keeping things in the family, my younger brother, Jack, became a boatman for Dave. When he wasn't running boats, he was studying materials science at Utah State University. He realized that the bags and sleeping pads the river companies were using could be made better. Back then dry bags were heavy, black rubber, army surplus bags with awkward closures, and sleeping pads were simply a piece of foam and a sheet of Visqueen. Jack started making high-quality dry bags and waterproof sleeping pads out of PVC material. They were a hit, and he started his own company. A few years later he also started making boats. They were a hit, too. Soon most everyone in the small, tightly connected river running community wanted what he was making.

My own story of getting addicted to river trips is also common: Once I'd had a taste of life on the river I was hooked. Since that first trip down the Grand Canyon, river trips have been a constant part of my life. At first, I would join trips with my brothers. Then in 1983 I bought my first boat – from my brother, of course! Over the next few years, I took advantage of the different boats that Jack was designing and bought six more. With a fleet at my command and all the equipment to go with it, I started organizing my own private trips. I still did trips with my brother and his friends, but also with work friends, The Wasatch Mountain Club, and anyone who would go on my permit or invite me on theirs.

In 1998 I met Martha at the takeout for Desolation. We'd all had a rough trip. The afternoon winds in Desolation Canyon are notoriously difficult, but on this trip, they blew more than forty mph for thirty-six hours! Martha's battery was dead, and she needed help getting her truck started. While someone was scrounging up jumper cables, we talked. Martha had run into a couple of young girls who were not prepared for the strong winds. Their boats had flipped, and they lost all their food. Martha helped them right their boats and then invited them to join her trip. As it turned out, Martha had met my sister-in-law, Lauri, the year before. Lauri told her that she should get together with me because we were both older gals who loved river trips. Martha and a group of ladies who were guides on the upper Colorado did a ladies' trip every year. She invited me on her next trip, and I've been on a ladies' trip at least once a year ever since.

Desolation on the Green is my favorite stretch of river, despite the winds and its infamous mosquitoes. When we first started doing Deso, we'd get permits around Pioneer Day, the July 24th Utah holiday, so we could use fewer vacation days and take advantage of the three-day weekend. But that's the worst time for mosquitoes! On one trip they were so thick you couldn't see the color of your cooler. We started scheduling our trips earlier or later . . . and brought bug nets to wear on our heads just in case.

The first day on Desolation, before you get into the steeper part of the canyon, the water is slow. It's a slog to get to the nicer camps downriver. Commercial trips motor the first twenty-four miles of the trip. But by motoring, they miss that first great blue heron flushing from the bank then flying downstream and, perhaps, the grazing horses at Wild Horse Canyon. Oh, do my muscles ache in these older years on that long row! But it's worth it to get a favorite camp at Gold's Hole or Stampede Flats.

In the thirty-seven years between my first and last river trip down Desolation and Gray Canyons, there have been many changes. The non-native tamarisk bushes have come and mostly gone thanks to the tamarisk beetle introduced a couple of decades ago. Now it's possible to camp once more in the friendly willows and grasses at House Rock and other side canyons instead of fighting for a nest among the nasty, bug-infested tammies. Two years ago, we hiked into that canyon and found the eagle's nest on a cliff face that my brother, Dave, had pointed out years before. It's a little bigger now, the eagles adding to it every time they use it. Rapids I used to scout that almost made me pee my pants in the early years have been washed out in flash floods and now have mild waves in high water and fun rock dodges in low water. Camps that we had to squeeze ourselves into have become luxury suites with cottonwood trees to hang hammocks and flat, sandy spots just right for a tent and pad.

Scouting Coal Creek Rapid on Desolation,
Green River, Utah

I've changed, too. But the peace and beauty surrounding a desert river keeps me coming back. After all the coordinating and rigging for each trip, I love the feeling of finally pushing off and floating quietly without a stroke as the current embraces the boat and gently glides it down river. I notice the dragonfly trying to get a ride on the tip of my boat tube, and the gentle sway of the grasses along the shore. On shore I love the predawn feeling when the dark sky slowly begins to lighten. The birds wake and call out to each other. Then I hear my companions clinking pots in the kitchen as they prepare that first, coveted cup of coffee. There's nothing like a morning meditation at the river's edge with a warm cup of brew in my hands as I watch clouds skim across the canyon, or a beaver swimming upstream as friends talk about the upcoming day on the river.

Flips tend to disrupt such reveries – and I have flipped plenty of times. I only flipped my big boat once in an innocuous rapid on Split Mountain called School Boy. My new Bimini shade top caught the wind and slammed the left tube into a ledge on the wall and over I went. In my smaller boats, I've flipped in several of the most dangerous rapids: Hell's Half Mile and Upper Disaster on the Green, and Satan's Gut and Big Drop Two on the Colorado. My belief, as I tumble through the rapid, is that if I flip, I will survive. It's paid off. I've always calmly made my way to shore or to one of my friend's boats.

Low-water Trips

There is a reason my nickname is "Low Water Nancy." I have a special feeling for low water trips, which require a certain amount of flexibility – both mentally and physically. Some of them are more like backpacking, but instead of hiking with a pack on your back, you're hopefully floating but often dragging a boat downstream. Backpacking experience does help minimize gear and food and make lugging your boat a little easier. Even though I love the comforts of camping with all the gear I can carry on my big boat, it isn't a problem getting comfortable with much less. On my little boat I've floated the Dirty Devil, Muddy Creek, the Escalante, the Price, the White River, and recent San Juan River trips that could qualify as low water trips.

Often low water trips involve an element of the unknown. When I dragged the Escalante River in 2002 with a few friends, a map of the river didn't exist. We took a "no whining" vow as we pushed off in ankle-deep water. There was not a proper guide for that stretch back then, so we used USGS topo maps and a diary from someone who had done the trip a couple of years before. We had seven days to go the seventy miles from Calf's Creek bridge to the mouth of the Escalante Canyon where my husband, Gailen, would meet us with a power boat and tow us to the takeout on Lake Powell.

It was a challenge. We pulled and dragged our little catarafts from dawn to dusk to complete the journey on schedule. And there were other challenges. We encountered a four-foot black bear near Fence Canyon. Luckily it wasn't that interested in us and disappeared over the hill. Then we ran into a man named Robert just after we passed Steven's Arch. He had launched two days after we did in a $100 Sevelor raft with a milk jug of water and a few power bars. He was on a soulful journey, trying to reconcile why his girlfriend didn't want to get married. He had left the river at Escalante Wash where he had to climb up through The Crack, but he had no idea how he was going to get back to his car. We took his boat with us, gave him my address, and said to come pick it up whenever he could, wondering if we'd ever see him again. We later learned he made it, getting a ride from a couple of guys he met on his hike out. They were suffering from dehydration, and Robert literally had to carry them up the 1,000-foot mountain of sand to get them to the canyon rim.

The Escalante was epic. The thorny Russian olives were so thick that we ducked behind our coolers as we crashed through the trees. Towards the end of the trip as we approached a massive beaver dam, their slapping tails scared the daylights out of us. It took a few slaps to realize they were beavers not gunshots. Once we got past Coyote Gulch we were in mudflats and had to drag our boats. Closer to Lake Powell the mud flats turned to quicksand, and we had to swim/shimmy across the top of the rocks, dragging our boats with us until we reached the lake. Finally, we were floating! What a nice surprise when Chris pulled out a beer. We passed it around, watching turkey buzzards soar with their shadows weaving patterns on the sandstone cliffs.

On one Muddy Creek trip, we ended up spending the night when we hadn't planned on it. That's when I discovered that an extra-large dry bag was big enough for me to sleep in. But it was too cold to sleep. We stayed up all night gabbing and telling silly jokes, trying to keep warm. The next morning, we floated around the corner and there was the truck. Ahhh . . . if we'd just gone around one more bend!

Martha and I once went down the Dirty Devil, just the two of us. We were doing our own shuttle, so we each drove. At the put-in we dropped our gear, rigged, and tied up our boats, then headed to the takeout where we would drop one car, and drive the other back to the start. At the takeout, Martha's truck got stuck in Poison Spring Wash. We thought about waiting for someone to come along and help, then tried digging the wheels out of the sand. That's when I remembered that I had a tow rope. We hitched the rope to Martha's bumper, and I easily pulled her out.

We never knew exactly where we were on that trip as we dragged and pulled our boats over the wide, shallow ooze of dark gray mud that is the Dirty Devil. After three days we finally found ourselves around the corner from Poison Spring Wash. We were a day early. We had time for a layover day, so we explored Happy Canyon. What a happy surprise! It's a fantastic slot canyon with curving sandstone walls that are so close together you can reach out and touch both sides at once. It felt like we were the only people who had ever been there. There were no footsteps but our own. We took off our clothes and bathed in the sun on a sandstone ledge. We hadn't seen anyone for four days, which somehow justified all our hard work.

Adventures on the river have enriched my life and shaped who I am. Even though I don't go on as many trips as I used to – and I now choose easier trips – I will always appreciate the quiet peace that I feel while slipping through the lazy water, the knot in my gut as I head down the tongue of a rapid, and my friends, the River Goddesses, as I join them for more trips down the western rivers we cherish.

A grinning Nancy... always happy on the river and off

Haikus
Doreen Sumerlin

Doreen Sumerlin lost her home to the East Troublesome Fire, which started in Grand County, Colorado, in the fall of 2020. With it went all her journals and old photographs, but not her memories. We're grateful to Doreen for reconstructing some of her river memories through this series of haikus.

Doreen is among the original women who started on these ladies' trips over thirty years ago. She recently retired from the Forest Service. On the river, she shares her love of the outdoors through her knowledge of biology, botany, and birds. We always appreciate her calm and logic, especially when situations or women get a little crazy.

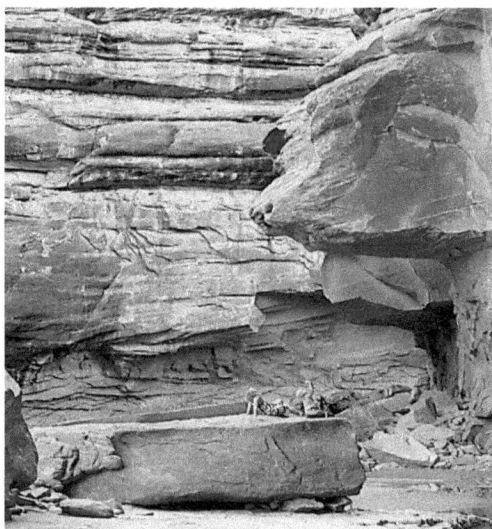

San Juan River: One
In Slickhorn Canyon
Orange, golden reflections
Women-draped ledges

San Juan River: Two
Little boats in line
Government Rapid punches
Motahari flips

San Juan River: Three
Twelve thirsty women
One shot of tequila waits
No one has the key

San Juan River: Four
Baja fogs at launch
A goddess celebration
Lime Creek dancing fire

San Juan River: Five
Distant roar and boom
Geometric shapes above
Surprise? Awe? Anger?

San Juan River: Six
Low water Nancy
Pull, push, paddle, walk, crawl, DANCE
"I'll sleep on my boat."

San Juan River: Seven
Bighorn rams crack horns
Herons glide downstream with teal
Goosenecks hypnotize

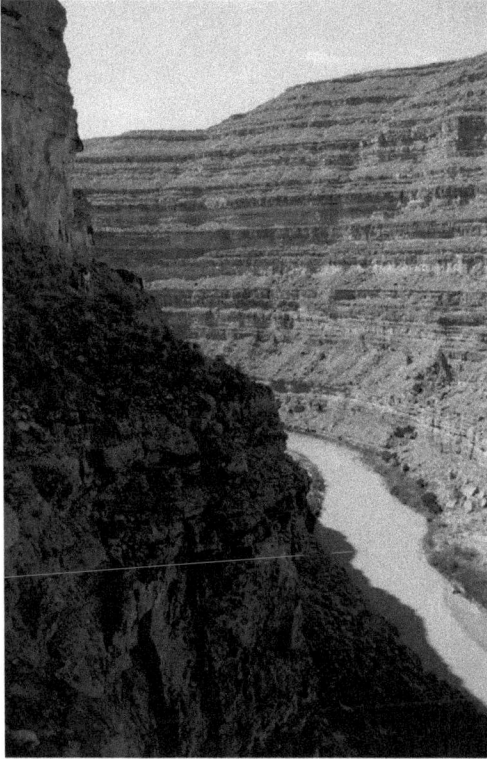

San Juan River: Eight
Up Honaker Trail
Brown ribbon-river below
Swallows dive and dip

San Juan River: Nine
Flash flood steamy hiss
Flip at Butler and Chinle!
Eddies swirl us in

San Juan River: Ten
Such a tiny beach
Ledge cocktail circle echoes
Long drop down to boats

San Juan River: Eleven
What, is that the wind?
Oh wait – it's the waterfall!
Once in a lifetime!!!!

Stillwater Canyon: One
Pink, rose, orange, tan?
Shadows dancing at sunset
Cobalt, indigo

Stillwater Canyon: Two
Pizza at Turk's head
Crawl through the slickrock tunnel
Camp site revealed

Stillwater Canyon: Three
Boats lashed stern to bow
O mighty W, please
Let us get to camp

Other Rivers: One
Permit maximum
How many women are there?
No one standing still

Other Rivers: Two
Naked sunbathing
"We didn't see anything!"
Yelled, falling from boat

Other Rivers: Three
Martha's wisdom sought
Whirlpools, Black Rocks protruding
"Spinner's a winner!"

Other Rivers: Four
Toilet lid flapping
While lashed to the stern cargo
Look, Jolly Roger!

Other Rivers: Five
Hurricane in gulf
Blue skies, fall colors, light breeze
And then the storm raged

Deso/Gray Canyons, Green River: One
Tornado warning
Heads in buckets as hail smashed
Blue, bruised tops of feet

Deso/Gray Canyons, Green River: Two
Prom dresses and gloves
Cedar Ridge painted bunting
Fremont petroglyphs

Deso/Gray Canyons, Green River: Three
Wet gear, wet kitchen
Lightning, squalls, dark stormy skies
"Gin'll help, ladies!"

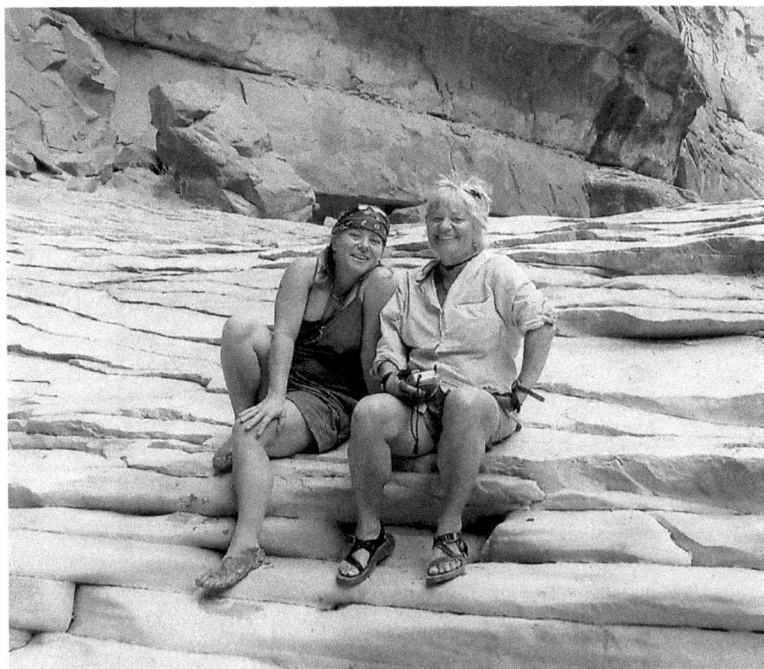

Deso/Gray Canyons, Green River: Four
Daughters and mothers
Grandmothers, aunts, sisters, friends
Generations merge

Deso/Gray Canyons, Green River: Five
All women hiking
Lonely cook with Mondo Biz.
"Eat it or Wear it!"

Deso/Gray Canyons, Green River: Six
Coal Creek kayak flips
Perfect Rattlesnake camp site
Nefertiti smiles

Sarongs and all rivers everywhere
Twisted, fringed and tied
Flowers, turtles, swirls and stripes
Lovely butt... erflies

A smiling Doreen on a ledge seat in
Grand Gulch, San Juan River, Utah

FLIP!
Zan Merrill

*Experienced boatmen say, "There are those who have
flipped, those who will flip, and those who will flip again."
Swift water rescue courses provide important information
and tools to draw on. But we can never anticipate the
circumstances in which we'll need to use them. Zan
Merrill tells a harrowing, high-water, flip and rescue
story.*

*As for the "those who will flip again" part of the saying:
Shelly, Ellen, Nancy, and Zan all flipped on other trips in
the following year or two. Zan flipped on two rapids with
the same name, Surprise, on Westwater and the Rogue;
Ellen against Tiger Wall on the Yampa and then in
Government Rapid on the San Juan; Shelly in Surprise
(those damn Surprises!) on Desolation; and Nancy in
Hell's Half Mile on Gates of Lodore.*

"**O**h! There's a Black phoebe. I'll add him to the
bird list . . . seems his lighter, graceful cousin,
the Say's phoebe, has headed south already."
My favorite river bird is the Say's with its gentle whistle
and subtle buff color, offset by a contrasting peachy
breast and dark wings. But my brief bird interlude is
interrupted by the immediacy and intensity of this river
trip. It's September 23, 2013, and the usually low-flowing
San Juan River in southeastern Utah jumped from 2,500
CFS to around 9,000 overnight. We planned this ladies'
trip thinking the river would be running at a normal level
for this time of year – less than 1,000 CFS – but launched
yesterday amid intermittent thunder showers and the
specter of dark gray clouds stacking upriver. Last night
Martha – one of the more experienced among us –
recommended that we double tie our boats with lines both
bow and stern to shore. It's a good thing we did. When we

woke the river was up two feet and our boats were floating several yards from shore, but there they all were, and they were easily retrievable with the extra lines.

Only an hour after we launched on the autumnal equinox there was a flip. Because there was so much water, we had decided to go down a channel that's usually too shallow to float, allowing easy access to a spectacular petroglyph panel with larger-than-life kachina figures. As we headed down the channel, Kelly lost her tarp when a gust of wind blew it off her boat. Sandra, always a trooper, went after it but didn't notice that the higher-than-normal current was cutting through a thick copse of thorny Russian olives that would usually have been up the bank a foot or two. I was behind her and watched the whole thing unfold in slow motion: the tarp billowed off Kelly's boat as she paddled clear of the Russian olives; Sandra watched the tarp hit the water and changed direction to intercept it; she swung her small cataraft sideways for a better angle, not realizing the trees were so close, and grabbed the tarp just as some branches snagged her raft – and she was over.

The first thing you do when someone is in the water is to try to get them out without complicating the situation or getting anyone else, including yourself, in trouble. I was in a good position to help. Sandra's upside-down boat swung clear of the trees and then she floated past them. I maneuvered to head her off, shipped my oars out of the way, and asked her if she was ready to get hauled into my boat, which is only slightly bigger than hers. I grabbed her by the shoulders of her life jacket and pulled her up and onto the gear in the front of my boat.

Sandra and I had been through this dance before on a Desolation trip a couple of years earlier. That time it was in the spring and the Green River was running high – 24,000 CFS. A couple of days before, we'd made it through Joe Hutch just shortly after it was newly excavated by a magnificent flash flood, which turned it briefly into a

Grand Canyon class rapid pushing IV on a I-V scale. Toward the end of that trip, we were going through some fun, usually forgettable rapids, when Sandra got caught sideways sliding into Sand Knolls Rapid and was overboard.

Back to the San Juan . . .. While I was rescuing Sandra, Kelly got the boat righted in shallow water near shore. The rest of the crew stopped to make sure everyone and everything was alright and, conveniently, they were at the trail head for the short hike to the Kachina panel. I dropped Sandra off at her boat. Doreen helped her get things back together and Nancy gave her some dry clothes. I rowed down to fetch the lost paddle, pulled over and hiked it back up. What happened to the tarp? I don't remember, but the petroglyphs were beautiful. The low autumn sun was just right, highlighting the contrast between the rock art and the rock itself. It's impressive and humbling to stand in front of a solemn, stylized figure bigger than you are, that was hacked into the sandstone hundreds of years ago. This panel boasts several large Kachinas – wide-shouldered, big-eyed, horned, hooded – and many smaller renderings of bighorn sheep, men, footprints, and snakes. Who knows what the Ancient Ones were depicting with the interspersed zigzags, spirals, and geometric shapes? The river perhaps.

That was yesterday. Today we're all a little edgy floating on this high water. This morning after we cover a couple of short miles, the plan is to pull into Chinle on the Navajo side of the river. We've obtained a permit to hike up the canyon. It's a delightful hike. We'll check out the Indian ruins perched high on the cliff and then ponder a pictograph that a friend calls the Baseball Man. He's particularly interesting because the carved petroglyph of a man is covered in a round, reddish and white, painted pictograph, which encircles him from shoulders to toes.

There are eleven of us on this trip, each in her own boat. The catarafts range in size from small-to-midsize, from

108

twelve feet long with sixteen-inch tubes and a narrow frame, to fourteen feet long with twenty-inch tubes and a wide frame. Janette has engineered her own "three-titted" raft with three small, twelve-inch tubes that are eleven feet long, and Mel's paddling an inflatable kayak (aka duckie). It's quite the fleet. Our experience ranges widely, too. A couple of gals started as guides in the eighties. A couple of others have boated most of their lives. A few have quite a bit of experience and are very comfortable on the water. Others come and go as they can on these trips and have varying levels of experience and confidence. I pulled the permit for this trip, which means I won a lottery drawing in March after throwing my name and a small fee into the hat in January. Officially that makes me the Team Leader, but this group is generous in sharing ideas and opinions, needs, and wants. That makes it easier to make decisions about the where's and when's of a trip: where to camp, when's the next rapid – around this corner or the next, how long is the Honaker trail, shall we stop for lunch or float and try for a layover day?

This morning Karen is in the lead as we head for Chinle Canyon. She's one of our strongest boaters and will decide if the pull in for the canyon is even possible. There's pretty good current where we need to get over. The river there runs in a straight shot along a steep, cobbly bank. At this level there won't be an eddy. It'll be difficult at best to get all of us in. At the last minute, Karen decides the pull in isn't possible. She swings back into the current. Kelly is following her too closely and is not able to get away from yet another bunch of trees dragging in the water. The same thing happens to her as happened to Sandra yesterday. Her boat gets caught by the trees, and she's over and in the water. I'm running sweep. That is, I'm at the back riding herd on this bunch and keeping an eye on things. I watch as the scene unfolds. Janette on the stable, three-tubed boat gets Kelly out of the water. That's good. Karen has grabbed the upside-down cataraft and is holding onto the bow line. Doreen has grabbed and secured a couple of things floating by. "OK, girls, now get the boat flipped over," I think to myself.

We are very quickly coming into the first canyon of the San Juan. The river narrows and speeds up even more between its tall walls. There will be no eddies to allow us to pull over and regroup like there were yesterday . . . at least not for several miles. But nothing more is happening up ahead. Kelly's not trying to right her boat and no one's moving in to help. I think I understand why. The situation is stable now, but not everyone realizes what's coming up. Once we're in that canyon it'll get tough for Janette to maneuver with another person on her boat, and it could get complicated for Karen to drag that flipped cataraft in this swift water. It's time to take action.

I swing backwards into the current so I can pull hard and catch those girls. I practically leave a wake as I stroke by everyone but Karen. As I approach Janette and Kelly, I holler, "Can you catch my bow line?!" Janette acknowledges, "Yes." I can see Kelly's tubes are skewampus, with one level at river line and the other at an awkward angle. My best chance to flip her boat upright is to jump onto the tube that's in the water, grab a strap on the other tube, and use my momentum to swing it upright as my own boat floats by. Damn! If this works, someone should be taking a video of this 61-year-old woman attempting such an acrobatic, athletic rescue. But there's only a second to fantasize heroics. Timing is critical. I toss my bow line to Janette, and she catches it. I position myself to jump. I clear my boat that Janette is skillfully rowing out of the way. As I land squarely on the tube of Kelly's cataraft I swing forward and grab a strap sticking up above the other tube. Leaning back with my full weight, I pull hard on the boat. It follows me over as I slide off and plunge into the water. The boat's upright! I grab the frame and haul myself into the seat. Kelly's cat is a paddle craft and I'm a rower. I hate paddling, but here goes. I tell Kelly to jump on my boat and start rowing to relieve Janette. She's shaken up and barely makes it. I holler at Karen to look for an eddy so we can pull in and regroup. Then I shout at Doreen and tell her to pass it on down the line, "We're going to pull into the first eddy we see!"

There's only one eddy and it's a doozey. It's immediately before we enter the canyon on the left-hand side of the river. The "eddy fence" is two, maybe three inches high. This is where the current in the eddy, which is going upstream, passes along the downstream current of the river. On this river, eddy lines are usually subtle and smooth – simply a change in the direction of the water as it flows past something as small as a rock or as large as a canyon. This eddy looks like a whirlpool – big, strong, swirling fast, and full of muddy froth. Lots of debris has been lifted from the edge of the rising river, mostly wood and branches, some Styrofoam and plastic, but also a tire, a derelict freezer, an old gate with big rusty nails sticking out of it, and a huge branching cottonwood log twice as long as our boats, that rhythmically sinks, then pops back up as it circles around. At least there isn't a dead cow in the mix.

The best place to catch an eddy is at the bottom or top. Most of us catch the top not wanting to venture to the bottom and miss pulling in altogether. Everyone gets in, a few crashing in at the top, through the strong fence line. Then we start circling – some go around the eddy several times before making it to shore to tie off their boats. Phew. Nancy's concerned about her daughter, Kelly. Kelly's shaken. Janette could use a break. Doreen's drained after chasing the floating gear. I'm pumped full of adrenaline. Everyone needs a chance to catch their breath. I decided a hike up the wash would be a good way to burn up some energy. A few joined me. At the top of the wash my companions turn around. I take my chances, do a little scrambling and rock climbing, and make it down the next wash. As we pulled in, I had noticed this wash just downstream. It was a steep drainage but connected to our eddy by a narrow bank that I could inch along to get back to the boats and join the others.

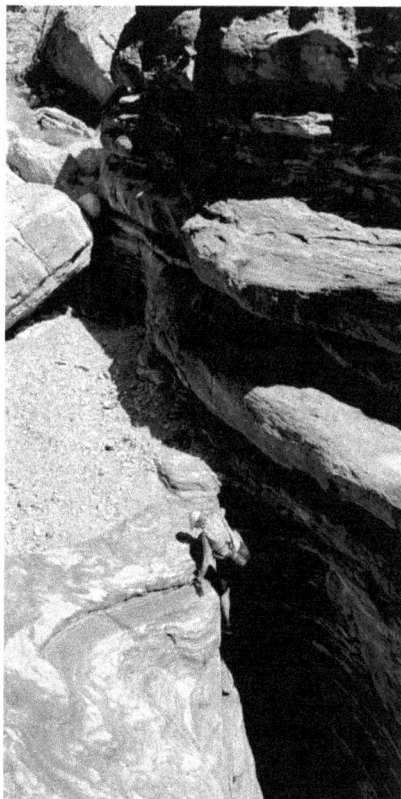

Zan climbing up a side canyon

After about an hour and a half, everyone had plenty of water and a little snack. Kelly's feeling better. We've gathered our wits and are ready to play dodge the debris and get back on the river. It's tricky. Martha goes first. She's so concerned about missing the bobbing gate with its nasty nails that she catches the cottonwood. It pops up just as she pushes off and lodges in her frame. She circles a couple of times, jumping up and down on the cottonwood trying to dislodge it. No good. On her next time around, I and I don't remember who else, wade out to meet her. The two of us grab the cottonwood and climb up on it. Using our legs, we start pushing it up and down with all our might. After building up some momentum, it's enough to get the branch free of Martha's frame. We get off the log and back to shore. Martha clears the eddy and disappears like a rocket down river.

The San Juan has a slightly steeper grade than most of the Colorado Plateau rivers, whose average flow is about three miles per hour (mph). With all this water I'll bet the San Juan's pushing eight mph. That's fast. Everyone else manages to avoid the tree and other debris and soon we're all racing down river. Our goal is Eight Foot, a camp next to a rapid bearing that same name.

Even with all the excitement we get to camp early. The rapids we're expecting – Four Foot and Eight Foot – are washed out at this level. We're relieved to be at the tail end of such a consuming and tiring day. We pull in and get ourselves settled unpacking gear, setting up a communal kitchen, selecting individual camp spots, and Karen, as always, finding a place for the groover. The afternoon's hot. It didn't take long – only a day – for it to warm up after the rains that caused the river to rise. I'm tired now and look for a spot to nap. I lie down under the dappled shade of some Coyote willows with just my sarong tied around me and my water bottle for a pillow. I close my eyes, but my senses are still heightened. Instead of sleep, I feel the cool sand against my arms and legs. I feel a fly light on my knee, an ant skitter across my shoulder, the drape of the sarong on my neck. In the distance I hear my friend's voices, the splash of ladies bathing in the river, the sound of water rushing by, and the wind, the typically incessant up-stream wind now a gentle breeze blowing across my body. Do I sleep? I don't know. But I'm content . . . happy that everything turned out okay today. Proud to be part of this group of women and proud of them – their judgment, quick responses, strength, help, compassion, and caring in a difficult circumstance.

Fifty-Five on the Gunny
Virginia (Ginny) Pizzella

Sometimes river trip adventures have more to do with the off-river parts of the trip than the river itself. To celebrate her birthday, Ginny Pizzella and Martha Hut ventured into unknown territory and had some unexpected experiences on what they came to refer to as their "urban river experience."

Ginny Pizzella is petite, but she packs a punch. She's as tough and strong as they come. Ginny landed in Winter Park, Colorado, where she started a landscaping business and drives snow-cat tours in the winter. One of the regulars on our ladies' trips, she rows a thirteen-foot self-bailer, while the rest of us row catarafts. If you're ever at a loss for something, Ginny probably has it, from the occasional bottle of good red wine to a pack of Via to stout up your coffee. Ginny's a huge asset on our river trips – pragmatic, efficient, and sure. She's serious when she needs to be, but she's also the first to kick back and have fun.

"I am an old woman named after my mother." So go the familiar opening lyrics of John Prine's *Angel from Montgomery*. Well, I really am! Sometimes I'm jokingly known as my mother's second son. I've always been a tomboy. I can still hear mother telling me, "Be careful! Don't take any chances," as I'd swing out the door with my roller skates. Somehow, I got past her Catholic notion of fear. But there were also my father's expectations. As a woman of Italian descent, I was supposed to marry a Catholic and have Catholic children. That vision of a successful life path just didn't seem to fit. My path led elsewhere.

Growing up in our small New England town during the sixties and seventies, the seeds were sown for my love of the outdoors. We spent a lot of time outside. There was biking and hiking in the summer and ice skating in the

114

winter. Mom enrolled my sister and me in an after-school ski program. That's when my love affair with sports and nature really started. I loved the thrill of speed skiing down the mountain. The sunlight glistening and sparkling off the snow was mesmerizing. The way freshly fallen snow draped the pines and hushed the entire landscape enchanted me. I had to make skiing a part of my life. Becoming a Phys Ed teacher seemed a means to that end. Sure, there'd be lots of indoor classes, but I could also teach skiing in the winter and tennis in the summer. Right? Anything to be outside.

After high school, I moved to the White Mountains of New Hampshire to follow my dream. There my playground broadened. It felt like I had found my place – at least a place to start – and I had chosen my way of life. I learned that a lot of those Catholic sins I'd been warned against were, for most people, simply living, and that included dating people who weren't Catholic. Marriage came twice with men who shared my love of the outdoors and not my religion. I never became a Phys Ed teacher, but I taught yoga and of course skiing as I maneuvered my way out West.

Rafting

By the time rafting was introduced to my long list of outdoor pursuits, I was living in the Colorado high country. One of my early experiences with boating was on a paddle boat with a bunch of men. We were trying to bust through a class IV rapid and the raft dump trucked – the boat stood on its side as it hit a huge wave – and everyone fell out except me. Yep, I was the only one left in the boat with my paddle wondering, "Now what?" I decided that the problem with being a passenger is that you're just a passenger! I wanted to be in charge. I wanted to row my own boat.

Where *are* your men? The truth is, back then I was always with men. I thought I was a strong, independent woman keeping up with the boys. But I was holding back, unsure and, yes, afraid. It took time to gain confidence and the real strength that I needed. Over twenty-five years rafting, I learned about river life and real life – the good and the not so good. Finally, when my second relationship unraveled, I knew I had to do things on my own, including being my own oarswoman.

That's when I thought of my friend, Martha. I admired her. She'd pack up and go on river trips without her husband. She was self-sufficient on the river. We had been on several river trips together and we mixed with the same crowd. It was about the time my second marriage broke up that she introduced me to an amazing group of women boaters. It was then I knew I had finally found my tribe. In the years that followed these ladies enriched my life and most certainly helped me to row my own boat in more ways than one.

The Gunny

I was turning fifty-five – double fives. Not a hugely significant birthday – not old, no longer young, not exactly a milestone – but I wanted to celebrate my independence. I'd taken over the thirteen-foot Aire raft that my ex and I bought together and made it my own. I wanted to work out the kinks – make sure I had everything I needed, that I could handle the logistics and could do a multi-day river trip without anyone's help.

My birthday is in the fall. In the Colorado mountains it's a busy time of year with people tidying up their yards for winter or trying to get one more trip in before the snow flies. I asked around, trying to find someone to float with me down the Gunnison for just a few days. The only taker was Martha. Perfect. There'd be two of us on the Gunny.

The plan was to go from Delta, Colorado, to Redland Dam near Grand Junction, a float of about forty miles. Usually, people run this section, which goes past the Dominguez Canyon Wilderness Area, in three days, but we decided to take four and tack on a few more miles upstream. That would float us past some homes, farms, and ranches and make part of the trip an urban boating experience. We made our plans, packed our gear, and headed out.

One of the things you learn about river trips is to expect the unexpected not only on the river but when getting there and back. It helps to be flexible, patient, understanding, accommodating, and sometimes cautious. To start the trip, we left the mountains and headed down to the desert. Our driving schedule was a little tight and, wouldn't you know it, right before we hit I-70 we had to wait for a herd of cattle to cross the road before we could continue west. They seemed to come out of nowhere, plodding along at a maddeningly slow pace. We finally did what anyone with western driving experience does and carefully, slowly drove through the herd. We were still mostly on schedule.

That night our goal was to camp near Delta, Colorado. The place we'd planned on camping appeared to be a designated campground on the road map, but in reality, it seemed to be a transient encampment. It was more than a little sketchy for a couple of gals to camp there. When we asked the woman camp host about tent sites, she seemed amused. In the lady's room there was a sign that stated, "No hair color in sink." We couldn't help but get a chuckle out of that. I'm sure the several men who were "camping" there wondered about the two crazy older women with rafts. What were they doing pitching tents in the middle of what appeared to be their dog-relief area? I wondered myself but we didn't have a Plan B, so I tied the inside zippers to my tent shut knowing full well that the nylon walls offered only a thin layer of security. All we could do was hope for the best. Sleep was fleeting thanks not only to our concerns, but also to a very happy and active couple not far away. All I could think about was getting out of this campground and on the river.

The next morning, we got going very early, which gave us plenty of time. We decided to drive the hour to and from the takeout to get our bearings and confirm exactly where we needed to get off the river. Our shuttle driver had told us that leaving my truck in Delta may be risky, but it was riskier still leaving it at the takeout. We had to agree, but what options did we have?! We needed my truck at the end of the trip so we could pack up and head home. Parking for the takeout was basically an isolated turnaround near the Redlands Dam with yet more transient camps not so hidden in the willows and trees. The takeout itself was nothing more than a slip just past some bushes, barely wide enough for our little boats to get into one behind the other. We marked an upstream cottonwood with flagging so we could find the slip when we floated by in a few days. We headed back to the launch, crossed our fingers, and hoped the truck wouldn't be broken into at the takeout when the driver dropped it off a couple of days later. We were starting to wonder about our choice of rivers.

We got back to the launch mid-morning and rigged our boats. As with all river trips, once we pushed off, all that mattered was the river – our concerns were left behind and we were on river time. The first two days were more than pleasant as we floated through scattered homes and ranches. The fall colors were just peaking, highlighted by the subtle, indirect light of autumn. Fields were golden with hay put up in various fashion – traditional bales that could be pitch-forked, huge bales that needed a forklift, and big rolls intermittently scattered across the fields. Cows were settling in pastures after roaming summer range up in the hills – possibly the ones that blocked our earlier path? Wood was cut, split, and neatly stacked next to houses. Winter wheat was sown. We camped those nights on sand bars so as not to trespass on private property, enjoying the stars accented in clear, crisp air. We woke to frost in the morning but basked in the slowly warming, bright autumn days. We shed layers of warm clothes till we got down to t-shirts and shorts by afternoon, only to don them again when the sun disappeared.

On the third night – my birthday night – we took a layover in beautiful Dominguez Canyon. It's named after Atanasio Dominguez, one of two Franciscan friars who explored the desert southwest in the late 1700s. Interestingly, they never made it to this canyon as they worked their way north into Utah. It was named by Ferdinand Vandiveer Hayden as part of his expedition to map the West Slope of Colorado in 1874. Hayden is notable from a rafter's perspective as being John Wesley Powell's main competitor to be the Director of the U.S. Geological Survey after they both established themselves as explorers in the western U.S. – Powell on the Grand Canyon and Hayden most notably in Yellowstone. Powell became the director and a river legend while Hayden all but faded into history.

Beautiful Dominguez Canyon offers considerable contrast compared to many canyons of the southwest. Geology ranges from ancient dark schist topping a billion and a half years old to much younger red rock sandstone not even half a million years old. Petroglyphs span epochs, from the Archaic style of 1,000 B.C. with etched deer, elk, and anthropomorphs to the Ute style ending in the late 1800s with men on horseback hunting buffalo. Pioneer ruins punctuate the path that winds up the main drainage. We enjoyed everything the canyon had to offer. We hiked in red rock, sweet sage, and rain. That night we saw meteor showers. We absorbed all the sights and sounds the wilderness had to offer.

If that wasn't enough, Martha gave me a child's charm bracelet with plastic turtles for my birthday. She had found it at the put-in and tucked into her pocket. It was wrapped in a bandanna – a useful piece of clothing on a river trip that can be worn or washed with – and tied with a piece of nylon cord that I knew would come in handy at some point. The gift was accompanied by tequila shots as we laughed over the shaky start to our trip and wondered how it might end. It was a perfect celebration!

On our last day as we floated out of the wilderness area, we found ourselves back on the urban river. We rowed out past more homes, alongside a road, and under overpasses. As we floated around curves towards the dam and takeout, we looked for the marking tape that we had tied to the tree. There it was. We slipped into the narrow takeout and went looking for my truck, hoping it would be there in one piece. My Toyota was nowhere to be found! It seemed this trip wasn't going to have a good beginning *or* end. There was nothing to do but derig. We figured one of us could stay with the gear while the other walked the mile or so down the road to a commercial business and phone the shuttle driver. But lo and behold, as we were derigging the driver showed up! He had our backs and hadn't wanted to leave the truck where something might happen to it. All was well! We packed up and hit the road sure that we were well on our way.

About a half mile down the dirt road, we stumbled upon a potter's field. It was too interesting to pass up and seemed an oddly appropriate end to the trip. We pulled over. As we stepped into the cemetery, curious to read the few headstones, rounds of rapid-fire shots broke out! Now what!? Terrified, we ducked and ran. We had no idea what was happening. As we made our way back to the truck, we saw there was a police shooting range next door. OMG! We laughed with relief. This was going to make quite a story. Or was it? We piled back into the truck and pointed our wheels north wishing we didn't have to wait until spring for our next river trip. Back home when friends asked us about the Gunny, we looked at each other and winked. "It was a great trip. The perfect way to celebrate my birthday." We left it at that. The trip had been a little too bizarre to explain. As we say, "What happens on the river stays on the river."

Ginny ready for anything on a Grand trip

River Journal: Spring Trip, Deso/ Gray Canyons, Green River
Sandra Thorne/Brown

Journals can be the most in-the-moment, direct form of written expression on the river. Sandra Thorne/Brown shares one of her journals from a Desolation/Gray trip on the Green River.

A forester and lover of trees, Sandra was one of the earliest female foresters hired by the US Forest Service where, for the first few years, she had to wear a man's uniform! We can always count on Sandra to identify a tree species that we aren't quite sure of, or to point out a particularly lovely specimen of cottonwood, ash, or a rare species like a catalpa or fruit tree planted by a homesteader during the last century. Sandra lives in Pocatello, Idaho, with lots of trees, her husband, and her new golden retriever puppy.

Sitting on a perch twenty feet above the Green River, about sixteen miles below Sand Wash. Nancy says our camp is called Gold's Hole.

Arrived at Sand Wash on Friday: Four hours from Salt Lake City. Cold in SLC. Warm and sunny at Sand Wash. Fifteen women from Pittsburgh, Winter Park, Durango, SLC, and Pocatello gathered at camp before dark.

Saturday, on the river by 11:00 a.m. – latest departure any remember. In a strong wind, slow water became sheets . . . rolls of waves moving upstream against us by 1 p.m. We fought the current, cold wind, and scattered raindrops. Finally pulled over about six miles short of our goal. It's a lovely camp, high above the river. Wind carried sand, mostly below us. Set up tents because of the cold, howling wind.

Sunday brought clear skies that promised quiet waters and warm air, upstream winds, and great birding. Floated to Firewater Rapid where we camped for the night. I set up my bedroom beneath old crumbling cottonwoods, feeling sheltered and special. Then the ants moved in, and I moved out – near the camp kitchen, closer to the river. Someone loaned me a four-inch-thick Paco Pad. Can sleep on most anything now. No "Princess and the Pea" for me! Remembering last night's Dutch oven dessert of peaches, oatmeal cookies, strawberry sodas, and cake batter . . . splendid.

We hiked up the dry bed creek near camp. Reached a wee charming grotto at the top where we sat and found a seat formed in the rocks along the ridge. Several petroglyphs of rams on a wall near mouth of the creek.

Next morning was overcast and cool. Rose early, sitting beside the river. (Oh, good! Time to find the groover.) Floated two more hours to next camp. My room is near the river between tamarisk and young Fremont cottonwoods. Hiked about three miles up a side canyon looking for the arch and a waterfall. We found two small arches high on the ridge. No waterfall but a great hike beside perennial stream.

Nancy and I pulled over about a mile before camp. Short hike to the wall of spectacular petroglyphs, then an Anasazi granary (a pit about 3' x 4' on the ledge, with the top/entrance about a foot in diameter surrounded by a circular stretch of juniper).

Off the river on Friday. Enjoyed the fifteen strong, capable, kind, thoughtful, delightful, cheerful, caring, lovely women.

Sandra, shaded up in an alcove on Desolation/Gray

Deso/Gray Adventure
Jane Hansberry

*Paddling with a disability might sound like a challenge,
but it doesn't stop these women from paddling an eighty-
four-mile wilderness river. Jane Hansberry joined her
friend, also an amputee, on their first experience running a
river on their own, on individual inflatable kayaks.*

*Jane was one of the early participants in ladies' river
trips. Her Colorado outdoor adventures began in 1975,
when she came out from New England to race in the
National Disabled Ski Championships. Four years later
she moved permanently to Colorado, "coming for the
winters and staying for the summers." Her first river
experiences were on the Upper Colorado, outside of
Kremmling, Colorado, when she worked for the National
Sports Center for the Disabled in the summer of 1980.
Although Jane went on to float rivers in Idaho, Colorado,
Wyoming, and Utah, her outdoor interests have now taken
her in other directions.*

It was May 2004. The Green River was running 12,000
CFS – a solid spring runoff level. The trip was going
nicely, folks were getting along, the food was good, the
weather was nice, all was well. Best of all I was with my
good friend Mary Ellen. Like me she was an above knee
amputee. We met skiing in the mid-eighties and had
many adventures together on the slopes and off. We even
shared a mid-life adventure in our fifties, getting our
doctorates at the University of Pittsburgh. She got her
PhD in Rehab Science and Engineering, and I got mine in
Public Policy. Back in Colorado, we had been on many
women's river trips thanks to friends like Martha, Cindy,
and Meeche, who invited us to join them. Most of these
women lived in Grand County, Colorado, or had Grand
County roots and already knew us as skiers. On the river,
we felt immediately accepted and respected. We

appreciated the ease of communication, and the lack of judgment when we needed to ask for help.

On earlier women's trips we were passengers on other folks' rafts. This was our first experience running an entire trip on our own – in this instance the eighty-four-mile stretch of Desolation and Gray Canyons – in inflatable kayaks, aka duckies. We were learning a lot, thanks to Melanie, who was an experienced ducky hand. On the first day, I was struggling with how to rig my boat. Melanie walked by and offered to help. Thanks to her, I learned to "rig to flip," which turned out to be a valuable lesson.

For the first two days the trip was uneventful, except for the fierce, up-river winds. Several times over those days, we tied our boats together to take advantage of our collective strength rowing against the wind.

As the trip went on Mary Ellen and I got the hang of paddling our duckies. We navigated the bigger rapids well during the first two thirds of the trip – Steer Ridge, Chandler Falls, Joe Hutch, and Three Fords. But as we got into the last stretch with the biggest rapid of the trip – Coal Creek – we lost track of which rapid was which. We did not have a map and were relying on instructions from the other women. That had been working fine, but then somehow Mary Ellen and I got mixed up on two of the rapids – Rabbit Valley, an easy Class II rapid, and Coal Creek. To wit, we entered Coal Creek, the biggest, longest, and most technical rapid in Deso/Gray, thinking it was Rabbit Valley. Not good. We were at the top of Coal Creek, far over on the right. Ideally, given our skill level, we should have been river left to safely enter and maneuver through the rapid. Looking down river we could see the path we needed to take to thread a line between the canyon wall on the right and a big wave train that skirted a huge boulder with a big hole. We were in the wrong place. Uh oh.

But the three duckies were hanging together, Melanie, Mary Ellen, and me. Mary Ellen and I watched as Melanie executed a beautiful run. She threaded the needle between the canyon wall and the wave train. Next Mary Ellen entered the rapid. She was keeping her boat straight and then hit a monster wave, got sideways, and flipped. I watched and realized that I was likely heading for the same fate. The waves were too big for me to see much of what was happening, but I knew there were several big boats down river that would scoop Mary Ellen up. I later learned it was Melanie, in her little ducky, who rescued Mary Ellen.

My turn. I sat at the mouth of Coal Creek for a very, very long time. I wondered if I was strong enough to ferry across and miss all the waves. I had a crazy thought that maybe a helicopter could come get me out of the fix I was in – magical thinking for sure. I kept looking over to far river left, where Martha was hanging. A highly skilled boat woman, Martha had been performing "sweep" all week. It was reassuring to see her there as I knew she would be able to get to me quickly if I flipped.

At last, I took the plunge and headed into Coal Creek. I decided I would chance it in the wave train versus trying to thread the needle. The first few waves were OK, and I kept my boat straight. Then I hit a wave that knocked me sideways and I flipped.

After the shock of the cold water, I got on top of my boat and started trying to paddle my way down river. The current and the waves were buffeting me every which way and I lost my paddle. I remember saying out loud something like "OK, that's OK, let the paddle go and keep hanging on to the boat, you're doing great, good job, keep it up, doing great . . .." When I got rescued, the women who plucked me off my ducky thought there was somebody already with me because they heard me talking as I self-coached my way through the waves. My rescuers were the mother/daughter team Betsy and Nora from Durango. They threw me a line. I grabbed it and started pulling myself closer to them. It was smooth. Then Nora grabbed the ducky line, and I was alongside their big boat. It took a few tries and then Betsy and I coordinated a one, two, three, Heave HO! and I landed in their boat. As we made our way into the eddy at the end of the rapid where all the other boats were waiting, I was relieved to learn that Mary Ellen was fine.

Rafters and kayakers can milk every adventure and near miss for hours going over every detail and nuance of a run. Mary Ellen and I did just that between bites of lunch shivering from our time in the drink. But everyone jumped in with a "that's where I popped an oar!" or "I almost got sideways there, too!" We learned what happened with each person, each run, happy that we'd made it, and grateful for wonderful river friends.

A smiling Jane loving the Deso ducky trip

I Found It!
Beth Booton

We all lose things on the river. As we get older, the things we lose can be more important to our river experiences than ever. Beth Booton tells a story about a close call and a miraculous find.

A nurse practitioner, Beth does a fair amount of doctoring on our trips. If we'd wear our shoes in the nice sandy beach camps, there'd be far fewer injuries! But she always puts us back together. Beth is from the Midwest. After working and traveling in Southeast Asia with her husband she moved to Logan, Utah, where she raised a couple of sons and established her medical practice. Years ago, she started kayaking, which she still does, with the Logan River right outside her door. She added rafting to her interests more than a decade ago. We're grateful for Beth's skills on the river and off, her care, and her energy. Her exotic dinners are to die for.

O ne might guess I'd have a stupendous medical tale or two with my monster orange first aid kit and my professional background as a nurse practitioner. But because all the ladies consistently take such good care of themselves, my skills and my first aid kit are rarely needed. Thus, stories of serious rescue, suturing, bandaging, and splinting have yet to develop. There's an occasional splinter, scrape, or contusion that I take care of, but so far, that's it.

One little story unrelated to medical issues stands out for me, because losing things is a common occurrence while loading boats every morning on these trips. Things get temporarily misplaced in the hustle: a hat, sunglasses, a water bottle . . . you know. Finding my own wayward items makes me feel like a schizoid genius.

On a bright blue morning at our last camp, Rattlesnake Canyon, on the Green River a few years back, Martha suddenly noted she was missing a hearing aid! The hunt was on. You know those aids are pricey, minuscule, high tech, and often uninsured. Martha removes her hearing aids when on the water, but they go in her ears when in camp. When she started taking out her hearing aids that morning to get on the river, she noticed one was missing. My near vision is lousy, and I'm not great at finding others' lost items, but I started looking. As the search progressed, the device's demise in the river seemed likely. Nevertheless, I wandered away from the others searching the beach toward Martha's now empty campsite. I could see the imprint her tent had made in the sand. In a nanosecond of dumb luck and a strange air of Deja vu, I looked down at the edge of the imprint and instantly saw a one-centimeter wisp of a white, angel-hair noodle poking from the sand. I was certain it was a morsel of last night's dinner or simple beach detritus. But with just a gentle tug, the full device gloriously emerged unscathed. Martha was quite surprised and relieved as she tucked the aid safely away, adding she had been doubtful (as were we all) that it could be found. Somehow it started the day wonderfully and continued that way all the way through derigging at the take-out and driving home. A happy ending to a great trip.

Beth cleaning up Zan's foot after a minor injury as
Faye looks on

Daisy
Janette Diegel

River trips are almost always full of surprises. En route to the river, the ladies in this story discover and rescue a dog that had been hit by a car. Janette Diegel's love of animals is clear in this sad and hopeful story.

W e were driving down US-191 in the dark towards Blanding. It's a desolate section of southern Utah, but time flies by while catching up with friends on the most important things in life, like what we forgot to bring for our annual ladies' trip, or what each of us were fixing for our upcoming designated meal. The conversation flowed from one topic to the next like the river we were headed for, with rare pause. I love these trips. It's such a special time to connect with friends from at least three states, sometimes more. It's time to unwind, to re-energize, to center ourselves. We float in individual boats, yet each of us takes a role, and we make up a tribe.

Out in the distance, out in the dark, I see something in the road. OH, NO! A dog has been hit and is lying dead in the road. An advocate for animals, I have fostered over 100 dogs and at least as many cats. My mood changes from a happy buzz to sudden sadness. I choke back tears. I steer the truck around and say a little prayer for the unloved. For the discarded. For the forgotten. I would normally have stopped to say, "I'm sorry." Sorry for the life that ended in such a lonely place, alone. I would have taken the shovel from the back of the truck and buried the body. I would have said a passing word. This time I kept driving.

We were in a caravan of three vehicles, my truck in the center. We were meeting to float the San Juan River, a wonderful tributary of the Colorado River that flows through a remote section of southern Utah, bordered by the Navajo reservation on the south. Water in the desert is a magical life source. It's a wonderful place to visit, catch up, and unplug.

We arrived at the designated meeting campsite and hugged each of the first group, many of whom we hadn't seen in a year. The third vehicle was shortly behind us, so we started setting up camp for the night. We waited. And waited.

The third vehicle arrived much later. We were getting concerned that something might have happened, and we were starting to talk about retracing the route to find them. Mind you, cell coverage is spotty at best in the desert. Just as we were deciding what to do, they arrived. They had been delayed . . . by a dog. They opened the back door, and there, lying in bloody blankets was the dog that I had driven around. My heart skipped a beat. In their telling of the story, enough time had passed between when I drove by, that when the third vehicle passed the dog was wobbling down the road. It wasn't dead! I felt relieved, yet angry at myself that I hadn't stopped. The women had tried to find a shelter, or a place where they could leave the dog in good hands. They were told to, "Tie her up beside the road. Someone will come and find her." In the loneliest part of Utah!? In the dark? We don't do that to a pup in need.

Having just taken an emergency first-responder-for-dogs class – doesn't everyone? – I assessed the extent of her injuries. She was a small female pit bull, or "pittie." She was pretty banged up but didn't show signs of any major injuries. Such a relief! She must have fallen out of the bed of a truck and tumbled. Or was thrown out. Who knows? I've seen worse.

We pondered what to do. She couldn't come with us because of the river regs. We spent the next few hours trying to find her owner, or someone else who would care for her. The police had been notified. There wasn't anyone else to tell. The closest veterinarian was in Cortez, Colorado, which was an hour and a half drive. They wouldn't have allowed us to surrender an out of state dog. It was past 10:00 p.m. already. And we had a launch permit scheduled for first thing in the morning.

Daisy, the worse for wear after tumbling out of a pickup, but resting comfortably after her ordeal

We have friends in Moab, Utah, which is two hours back from the direction that we had come from. I called Arne, a fellow dog lover, and a fellow friend of most of the group. We were able to talk him into meeting us halfway and keeping the dog safe for eight days while we were on the river. How could he say no to a group of women friends? Especially THIS group. An hour later, we met Arne in a dark parking lot. I handed him a bloody dog – which I knew nothing about – and said, "Trust me. I'll get her when we're off the river." Then I got back in the truck and drove away.

The trip was all that ladies' trips are meant to be! Relaxing, fun, inspiring. We talked about what to call our newest member of the group, the little pittie that was waiting for us when we returned. We decided that, since pit bulls have such a fierce reputation, we needed to come up with a cheery name. Daisy? Yes! It fits. We passed a hat around, a collection for her medical and future needs. We weren't about to abandon a fellow girl in need.

When we pulled off the river and were in cell range, I called Arne. He had arranged to get Daisy back to Salt Lake and met me with only a few stories to tell. He had taken her to a vet. She wasn't microchipped, and she was lucky to have only minor injuries. She fit in with his own dog pack and was mostly trouble free. I will forever be grateful for this man and his compassion.

Since I had been a foster in dog rescue, I am quite familiar with what it takes to get a dog adopted. It's not easy to find a good home for a pit bull. But Daisy lived up to her name. She was the sweetest little dog – good with dogs, cats, kids, and people in general. Things fell into place as if they were meant to be. Best Friends, a rescue organization in Utah, happened to have sent out free spay-and-neuter coupons for pit bulls. Within two weeks, Daisy had all her shots, had finished healing, was spayed, and had time to show what a sweetheart she was. She was a new woman!

During this time, I had friends who were revising their landscape and wanted ideas and inspiration. I walked two houses away from our house and was talking to the contractor about the revisions they were considering. In a casual conversation, I mentioned that I had a pit bull that he should adopt. He wasn't in the position to take another dog, which didn't surprise me. But far be it from me to not talk about dogs in need of a good home. Two days later, he rang my doorbell. The guy who was working with him wanted to meet Daisy! Now, let me tell you my first impressions of this man: he was tall, well over 200 pounds of muscle and had a smile that would light up when you talked to him. I brought Daisy out to meet him and when

he dropped to his knees, she smothered him in
kisses. Sometimes the stars line up.

I kept in touch with Daisy's new dad for a while. She lived
on a small farm with goats, chickens, cats, and a human
who loved her. Daisy was one lucky girl. But no surprise
here. She was part of the ladies' river trip team. Enough
said.

"We Didn't See Anything!"
Cindy Southway

*On river trips, nudity happens – especially on trips with
all women. Even the best intentions to be discreet and
respectful of others can go awry. Cindy Southway tells
about the time two young men quietly stumbled on our
group of older ladies basking in their makeshift river spa.*

*Cindy was born and raised in Colorado. After graduating
from the University of Colorado Boulder, she moved to
Winter Park for a year to be a ski bum. She is still there.
She has worked for the ski area, the forest service, and a
land trust, and is currently self-employed as a non-profit
bookkeeper. Both of her sons are engineers and can row or
ski just about anything. Martha Hut introduced Cindy to
rafting in the early eighties. She is happiest on the water
and loves the rhythm, the solitude, and the excitement of
rowing her own boat.*

In the late nineties, after a long winter in the high
country of Colorado, a few of us ladies decided to head
to some warmer weather and raft the Gunnison River.
When we arrived at the put-in it looked like we'd be
enjoying some beautiful spring weather along with the
companionship and fun that ladies' trips offer. To kick the
fun off, we mooned a train from our boats as it went down
the track that follows the river for several miles. Who
knows what the passengers thought, but we all had a
good laugh. And, of course, we enjoyed the peace and
solitude that the river offers.

When we reached Dominguez Canyon after a couple of
days, we set up camp. Dominguez Canyon is the main
attraction on the Gunnison. Almost everyone stops to
walk up the canyon and enjoy the sights. We decided it
was the perfect spot to take a layover day. After breakfast
the next morning, we headed up the canyon on a hike. We
looked at the rock art, pondered the old pioneer ruins, and
admired the beauty of the canyon as we wound our way

up the trail. As the day progressed the temperature rose, and by the time we got back to camp it was a very warm afternoon. What a perfect day to set up a river spa! There was a big, flat, dry rock at the edge of the river with a tall rock next to it that was ideal for hanging a solar shower. The big rock also blocked the downstream wind which kept the chill off as we dried. A few of us were lounging around naked on the rocks after showering and slathering lotion to counteract the warm temps, lack of humidity, and silty river water desert rivers dish out. We were completely relaxed – chatting, snoozing, and rolling over every once in a while to even out our tans.

It was about 4:00 in the afternoon when, much to our surprise, a raft appeared seemingly out of nowhere. We hadn't heard it slipping quietly downstream. This raft had two twenty-year-old men on board. We recognized them. We had talked to them several times as we leapfrogged down the river. They covered their eyes and one of them yelled out, "We didn't see anything!" He was so flustered he fell out of the raft. We cracked up and were sure we had burned an imprint of aging, naked sunbathers into their eyes that they would never be able to forget!

The young men avoided us like the plague for the rest of the trip. We didn't see them again until the takeout at Whitewater Bridge. Our good weather had taken a turn for the worse and it was raining hard. This made derigging, which can be an intense and somewhat rushed chore, even more unpleasant than usual. We noticed that the young men were doing their best to keep out of our way. They seemed in a big hurry to pack up and get away from us old gals.

Jan backed her van down to load our gear and got stuck in the mud. The young men hid their embarrassment and graciously offered to help. They got behind the van and started pushing. Once Jan got a little momentum going, she hit the gas, but the tires spun out, covering the men head-to-toe in mud! We felt terrible. We knew how miserable they'd be sitting in their vehicle on the long ride home, so we unpacked our shower gear and handed it to them. They set up the shower in a discreet location, took a quick bath, changed into some clean, dry clothes, and finished packing. They never told us their names, but they took off south, maybe to Durango, while we headed north. I like to think that when they told the story to their friends, we all became very hot women in our twenties, and they *did* see something!

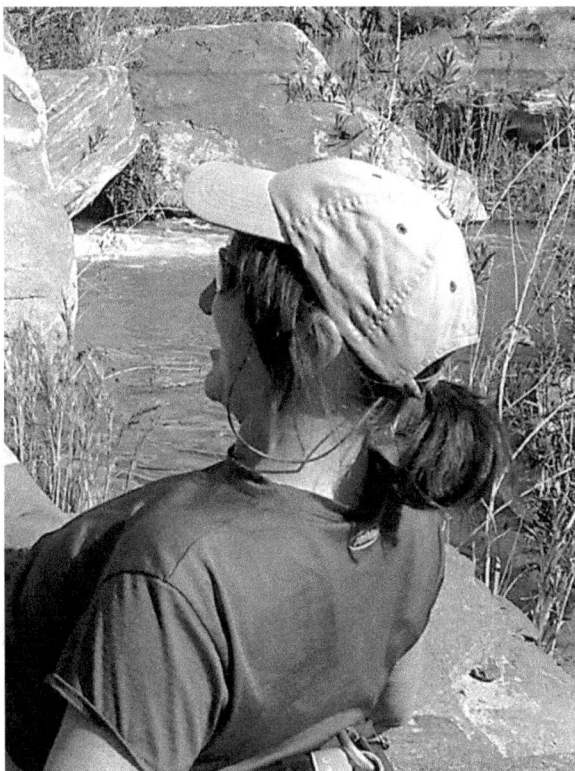

Cindy, relaxing and enjoying river time

A Collection
Karen Carver

*Karen Carver was a river guide with Martha Hut in the
Colorado mountains near Winter Park in the big-water
years of the early 1980s. She now lives in Durango,
Colorado, where she keeps busy doing a variety of
community-supporting jobs. Her big smile and never-a-
motion-wasted rafting style make her a joy to watch on the
river.*

*Karen instilled a love for the outdoors in her children. On
the river, she IS the Groover Queen with a routine no one
interrupts as she sets up the groover and settles river
water for our hand-wash systems and dish washing, big
chores that we all appreciate.*

River Spa Day Haiku

Shake and bake coating
Clay, sand, and river water
San Juan recipe

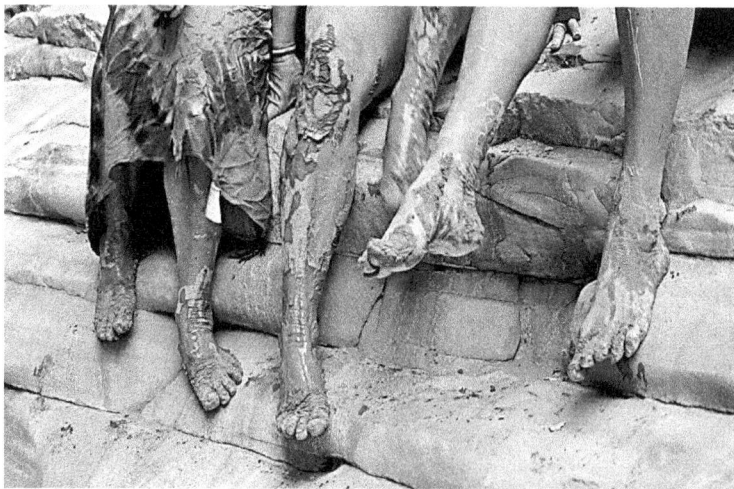

Mud-coated feet after a hike up Oljeto on the San Juan

Here's to Forty Years

One evening, still circled up in our camp chairs after dinner, one of the women asked me, "Karen, how long have you and Martha known each other?" I looked over at Martha, we shared a glance and some finger tallying. "Wow, forty years!" I marveled. Someone raised her cup and chimed in, "Here's to another forty years of boating!" "It will be so easy," said Nancy. The rest of us looked wide-eyed and puzzled, trying to imagine that. "No cooking!" Nancy continued, "All we will have to do is bring jars of baby food!"

The Groover Queen

"Last call groover!"

I get to say this every morning on the river. The proclamation either inspires a nonchalant "I'm groovy," or a bit of an anxious look if the urge hasn't arrived.

My role as "Groover Queen" began on a trip when there were eight of us and only seven dinner nights. I offered to do the groover in lieu of purchasing and cooking a meal. We always share expenses, so instead of food, I'd pay for groover supplies and cleaning afterwards. It would be a fair contribution to the group expenses.

I had just gotten a nice toilet system when I broke up with my steady – a going away present – and I was proud to show it off. The container is the same size as a rocket box, a twenty mm ammo can that measures seventeen inches by fourteen inches by seven and a half inches. It fits well on the back of my boat frame, out of the way but accessible during the day if needed. It can be the first item unloaded and the last one packed – very convenient. It's made of welded stainless steel so there are no leaky seams, and it doesn't deform in the heat like plastic can. Instead of a twist top with threaded grooves that can get icky, it has locking latches – very functional. I vent or "burp" it if it's really hot, but it usually stays cooler since it's down at water level under a dry bag where it gets splashed with river water, out of the direct sun. The seat is on a riser so there is a fifty-plus-use capacity, accommodating ten people for five days. There is nothing like a fresh groover halfway through a week-long trip, and if I need another can, my ex-steady and I are still on groover-speaking terms, so I borrow one of his.

At most river camps there are obvious kitchen and dining areas, dispersed tent or sleeping sites, and a groover spot. I judge the groover site carefully as to its suitability. One friend insists that you should be able to walk to the groover in the dark barefoot, which blends well with my criteria. There must be:

- Proximity to the water to facilitate disposal of liquid waste on desert rivers;
- A nice view;
- Some screening to allow for privacy but open enough to allow for airflow;
- A sandy surface for leveling or a flat rock in front to provide a firm platform for the feet.

As little pee as possible goes into the groover. As we age – especially for those of us who have borne children – keeping pee out of the groover can be a little difficult. A five-gallon pee bucket next to the groover offers extra comfort and convenience. I always make sure there is plenty of TP. But don't expect to find reading material; this is a place to do business.

I provide a mini orange cone as the groover flag. It can stand on its own in the path or be perched on the end of a branch, whichever is most visible. On larger trips, there may be several sets of eyes looking over to see if the groover flag is in place. If it is, the groover is open. If it isn't . . . well, you have to wait a little longer. Afterwards, you wash your hands well in the hand wash system that I also provide next to or near the groover. That was another present from my ex-husband.

Groover disposal is as easy as dropping the box off at our river sports store where the local port-a-potty company comes weekly for clean out. Sometimes I do the cleaning deed myself after short or small trips of up to twenty uses. Since my ex-husband and I are on groover speaking terms, I can use the sanitary dump at his house.

There used to be a self-serve dump station after taking off the Rio Chama in New Mexico. After one ladies' trip, a friend volunteered to help with the clean out. She had a traumatic brain injury after being hit by a car while bicycling and could no longer detect odors. As the contents were transferring from the groover into the cleaning vault, Maureen looked at me and said, "I think my sense of smell is coming back!"

After getting home, I always stow the groover restocked and ready for the next trip. I can be ready on short notice, so let me know and I'll bring the throne and be your "Groover Queen".

Karen, comfortable as always on her raft

My River Life
Elise Boeke

Sometimes life gets in the way, and we must take a hiatus from the things that keep us afloat. Elise Boeke relates her experiences on her first river trip after eight years away from the oars.

Everything Elise knows about rafting she learned through inquiry and observation. Her love of rivers and her quest for adventure gave her the foundation to figure out how to row. As a wildlife biologist, she is sometimes distracted by birds and other wildlife on the river. Elise is happy to identify the birds she sees and hears to fellow river runners, requested and unrequested. By the time she gets out of her sleeping bag in the morning, she's already identified half a dozen birds. Elise lives with her husband in a small, beautiful town in the northern Utah mountains. Her ready laugh and happy demeanor enhance any river trip she's a part of. We're glad she's back from her eight-year sabbatical and look forward to many more trips together.

I grew up in Oklahoma, playing in a creek next to the house chasing frogs and crawdads, spending hours exploring. It wasn't until I moved out West that I got the opportunity to get on big rivers. As a biologist for the Fish and Wildlife Service I sampled rivers – water quality, sediments, invertebrates, fish, and birds. My place on the rivers was to collect data, to learn what lived there, what was impacting these places, and how to protect them. I was in awe of these rivers: the Green, the Colorado, the San Juan.

My first big whitewater river trip was on the Colorado River through Cataract Canyon. I was a guest on a friend's boat. I loved lying on the bow of the boat, looking up at the cool blue sky and enjoying the warmth of the red rock as I floated on the ribbon of water running through the canyon. The isolation of the desert was intoxicating. Floating on the flat water the sounds are so clear: rock wrens chatter as we drift along, a raven croaks in the distance, and occasionally there's a swish as the oars push us forward. I hear the creak of an oarlock from another boat nearby. It's hot and the sun is intense. I slip into the water to cool down and float alongside the boat. The canyon walls are tall and seem to hug us into the river. At night the stars glitter, challenging me to stay awake to watch them move across the sky, but I'm too tired and my eyelids are heavy from the sun and laughter of the day.

The next day we approached a rapid. I heard it in the distance. I felt like I knew what was coming. I have many friends that are avid river runners, and I've heard countless stories of their adventures. I know about the rush of adrenaline. The water is powerful and not to be underestimated. I sat up and asked my friend to teach me how to row the raft. I listened. I watched. I learned.

Over the next several years, I was lucky enough to be invited on river trips that include some rock star river runners: boaters with countless trips through the Grand Canyon or Gates of Lodore – rivers known for their challenges; professionals – biologists, botanists, guides, geologists, geomorphologists – who made a living running rivers, experiencing waters demure and calm as well as explosive and roaring. I tagged along on rapid scouts, scrambling up sandy embankments that collapse as you climb, then up and over large boulders that have tumbled down the canyon walls, and through the scratchy mosquito-filled snarl of tamarisk to a place that overlooks a rapid below. I watched and listened. On a scout, people point to the lines they plan to follow and discern how they will maneuver their boat to miss a hole or avoid a pour over. They try to judge how pushy the river is and what it will take to deliver their boat on the other side of the rapid upright, tidy and with all the occupants safely inside.

Over the years I had more opportunities to get on more rivers and make more river friends – always generous with their gear, their experience, and their laughter. Finally, I invested in a boat of my own. It's a cataraft that's versatile: big enough to take on some big rapids and carry enough gear to be self-sufficient, but small enough to go on smaller rivers. She is blue and I named her Saphira, after the blue female dragon from the Christopher Paolini's book, *Eragon*. I like to think she is my blue dragon that carries me through the river safely with me at her oars.

I have mixed emotions on the river. I love the freedom of floating through the landscape. I love the peace, the solitude, and time to think. But I know that the river can be threatening, and the water can rise quickly and unexpectedly. It can push me and flip me and hold me down. I have to know how to read it and what it will take to move my boat where I want it to go. It challenges me to know what I can do and understand my limitations, while having confidence in myself and my capabilities.

Unintentionally I took sabbatical from rivers. My life got busy, my job was demanding, and my vacation time limited. It seems as though I looked up and suddenly it had been eight years since I was last on a river trip. Unbelievable! Then I got an invitation to join a ladies' trip and the stars aligned so I could go. I accepted with trepidation. It had been so long. Would I remember how to read water? Would my body perform for me and allow me to physically do what it takes on an eight-day trip? "Do it!" my heart said. So I did.

I had so much planning to do. Where was all my gear? Was Saphira ready to go? I pulled everything out. My gear was strewn across the lawn. There was cleaning, testing, prepping, making sure it was all ready. Then off I went to reintroduce myself to life on the river.

It was a small group of women going down the San Juan. I had been with them all except one on various other trips and it was wonderful to reconnect. It was like coming back to a family celebration, catching up on what had happened in our lives: partners and spouses and kids coming and going, new houses, wonderful adventures to hear about, and all the incidents and challenges along the way.

The river was low, at 500 CFS; none of us could remember the water here this low. It made for a boney ride. You had to pay attention, or you'd end up on a sleeper rock hiding just under the water surface. It was hot for a September trip. The only big rapid was Government – not much of a rapid as I recalled. The last time I did it, there were no issues. However, when we got out and scouted it, I felt anxious. It had been so long since I had rowed a rapid and at this water level all the rocks were exposed. My mind raced with everything that could go wrong. What if I flipped? What if I got pinned? What if I didn't have the strength to maneuver the boat through the only line that existed? I did NOT want to row it. Could I line it? Could someone else take my boat?

One by one, each woman left the scout and launched into the rapid. I stayed behind to watch what they did, how they positioned their boat at the top, where they dug in to pivot around a hole, where they were willing to go to avoid the huge boulder in the middle that would flip you if you didn't avoid it. As I watched each one maneuver the rapid my anxiety grew as I marveled at these women. They had such confidence! I knew this was NOT a big rapid by any stretch of the imagination. All these women had done much bigger rapids. *I* had rowed rapids bigger than this. These women gave the river the respect she deserved but they were not intimidated by her. I wanted to be in that place again.

I launched my boat and rowed out across the main channel to position myself above the rapid. The water was flat and slow. I stood up as my boat drifted on the flat water to confirm I was where I needed to be and looked for the marker rocks that would guide me through. "OK,"

147

I said, "This is it." I sat down, grabbed my oars, and followed the tongue into the rapid. I cocked my stern to the right, ready to pull around a big boulder, but not too soon or the water would push me into a giant pour over and into a hole where I would surely flip. My heart was beating wildly but I was smiling from ear to ear! When I popped out at the bottom, I whooped so loudly I'm sure everyone on the river heard me. I pulled onto the bank where the others were waiting for me and immediately started crying. I don't know why. I guess it was the release of the adrenaline and anxiety that had built up inside me. My friends met me with support and congratulations. These women gave me confidence. They mentored me and coached me. They shared their experience, their wisdom, and their laughter. They got me back on the river and *I* got through Government Rapid.

Elise maneuvering through low-water Government Rapid on the San Juan

All river trips are wonderful. I've never been on one that didn't leave me with a big smile on my face and amazing memories. This San Juan ladies' trip was no exception.

Elise, in a satisfied selfie after running
Government Rapid

River Time

Deborah Hughes

Morning slow dances
Down tumbled parapets
In a minuet of Moki steps,
Polishes desert varnish
With a new coat of day

The half-moon parachutes
Toward its dark phase
Across a pillow-pocked sky
Windowed by shadow-boxed rims

Moonflower reseeds downwind
In annuities of dangerous delicacy
Unfurls its nightshade
Into the numinous unknown

150

Century plants
Prove thirty reckonings,
Puncture the horizon
With blossomed bayonets

Chambered nautiloids
Spin around themselves
In Mississippian limestone.
Wetting their frozen faces
Reveals their circumambulation

Zoraoster granite
Awaits within the inner gorge
Beneath the greatest angular unconformity,
Has waited over 1.8 billion years

The river only knows
Now

Epilogue

We float through time on these western rivers – eons of the past, layer upon layer, rock upon rock. Just as we float through time, time floats through *us*. Although we've barely left a grain of sand as part of the geologic record, our lives have been richly layered with the shared experiences, emotions, beauties, and blessings that being on a river brings.

How long will we old gals be able to brave the elements, keep rowing, and deal with the challenges that river trips throw at us? As I read the adventures in this book, I think about how my – our – capabilities are changing. Already we're sending the more agile and limber among us down the river channel first when we know we're coming to a tricky landing so they can jump out, quickly tie a line, then help those with new hips and knees land their rafts. We've often joked about finding some strong young men – or women – to help us raft into our older years. It may not be such a bad idea. Any takers?

My cousin says that luck is what you make it. Most of the time I'm in agreement. Looking back at all the time we ladies have spent on rivers, I can't help but think that luck played a part, even though there's no doubt that we put a lot of effort into getting permits, planning, and organizing trips, maintaining our equipment, and staying fit. Whether it was luck or effort or both, it's been gratifying to spend as much time as we have on rivers.

How long *will* we run them? That remains to be seen. We'll keep rafting as long as fate allows. When that's no longer possible, we'll be happy for every memory and will cherish each moment that we spent adventuring on our beloved wild rivers with our dear friends.

Appendices

Appendix I
Glossary of Terms

Ammo Can – A waterproof, metal ammunition can originally designed for storing .50 caliber shells, which rafters use to store gear. Ammo cans are smaller than a rocket box (see below) and often used for easy access to items that the rafter needs frequently throughout the day, such as sun block, phone, a camera, and insect repellent.

Bailer – In non-self-bailing bucket boats someone must get the water out of the boat after the boat takes on water. That person is the bailer. Most modern rafts are self-bailing, so no bailer is needed.

BLM – The Bureau of Land Management is an agency within the U.S. Department of Interior that is responsible for administering federal lands, including many of the rivers that we run.

Boat – Technically this refers to a hard-sided craft. In fact dory captains get a little miffed about us usurping the term, but we take the liberty to refer to our inflated Hypalon or PVC rafts and catarafts as boats, too.

Boat Captain – The person running the boat, and often the owner of the boat. Her word rules while you are on her boat. Treat her with great respect.

Boney – Refers to conditions that feature rocks in the riverbed, often in low water flows. A flat section of river may be boney or a rapid may be boney.

Bucket Boat – A raft with a sealed-in floor. When water comes into the boat, it must be bailed out so that the boat doesn't get too heavy.

Cataraft – A boat construction that consists of two long, inflatable tubes strapped to a frame. Bailing is not needed.

CFS (cubic feet per second) – A measure of the volume of river flow. A cubic foot is the volume of a cube with all sides one foot in length. CFS is the standard unit of measurement of the flow of water. One CFS is equivalent to approximately 448.83 gallons per minute, yielding 646,317 gallons or 1.983 acre-feet of water in a 24-hour period.

Cutthroat – A 12-foot cataraft with 16- or 19-inch-diameter tubes manufactured by Jack's Plastic Welding, Inc.

Deso/Gray – Abbreviation for Desolation and Gray Canyons on the Green River. The put-in is at Sand Wash in east central Utah, and the takeout is near Green River, Utah. This remote stretch of river is about 84 miles long.

Double Duckie – A two-person/tandem duckie or inflatable kayak. See Duckie below.

Dry Bag – Dry bags are typically made of rubberized or water-proof nylon, polyester or vinyl with a roll top or zip lock-type seal to prevent water from getting into the bag. Clothes, sleeping bags, and other gear are packed in these bags to keep them dry.

Duckie – Also known as an inflatable kayak or IK, it's a small, narrow, inflatable watercraft typically propelled by means of a double-bladed paddle.

Duct Tape – Shiny, gray tape about two inches wide. Buy it in hardware or discount stores. Rafters use it for everything.

Dump Truck – The unfortunate situation when a raft or duckie tips on its side. Often the occupants are "dumped" out into the river.

Dunnage – The gear that is packed on the boat, including dry bags with your and others' personal equipment.

Endo – When a raft flips long ways, nose-to-tail.

Eskimo Roll – A complete rollover in kayaking, from upright to capsized to upright (performed in hard-shelled kayaks, not IKs).

Fat Cat – An 11-foot cataraft with 16-inch-diameter tubes, manufactured by Jack's Plastic Welding, Inc.

Ferry (upstream, downstream) – The most efficient way to get across a river, whether you're going upstream or down. A 45-degree ferry angle reduces the drag against your boat and allows you to deftly angle through the current to the other side, into an eddy, to meet another boat, or wherever you're going.

Flip – When a raft or other watercraft turns upside down in the water. Hopefully, you've "rigged for a flip" when it happens, or you're going to lose some gear. Sometimes occupants can get stuck under the raft, but more often they are thrown clear.

Groover – A river toilet: a waterproof container for your feces, usually fitted with a toilet seat. The name groover originates from trips operating back in the '70s, when you would poop right into a 20mm rocket box (no seat), leaving a set of grooves on your backside and thighs.

Hantavirus – A deadly virus carried by deer mice in the Southwest United States. Humans contract the disease by breathing in the virus through contact with the rodent or from its feces or urine dust.

High Side – The action taken by occupants of a raft or cataraft when the craft is rolling or tipping to one side. The occupants throw their weight to the high side of the craft to keep it from flipping, tipping, or dump trucking.

IK (inflatable kayak) – Also known as a duckie, it's a small, narrow inflatable watercraft which is typically propelled by means of a double-bladed paddle.

Lateral – A wave that approaches a raft sideways as opposed to straight on. It's best to hit big waves or waves that can potentially flip a boat as close to a 90-degree angle as possible. Setting up for laterals can be tricky; in many rapids a boater must be concerned with waves coming in from all angles.

Pack Cat – A small cataraft designed to be packable for hiking into remote rivers.

Permit Holder – The person who won the permit lottery for the trip. Without this person, there would be no trip. Treat her reverently. She obviously has good luck.

Put-in – The point of origination for a river trip where the boats are launched.

Rocket box – A waterproof, metal ammunition can originally designed to store 20mm shells, used to store river gear. Rocket boxes are considerably larger than ammo cans.

Roll – A kayak or Eskimo roll is the act of righting a capsized kayak with body motion and a paddle.

Safety Kayaker – The kayaker designated to ensure the other boaters are safe. Because kayaks are much more maneuverable than rafts or catarafts, it can be beneficial to include a safety kayaker, especially on more difficult rivers.

Scout – Scouts are performed before technical or large rapids. Boaters hike to a point along the river that provides a good perspective of the rapid. From there, they can assess the situation and plan the best line for getting through the rapid. Depending on the experience and confidence of the rafters, the length of the trail to get to the scouting point, and the difficulty of the rapid, scouts can take a considerable amount of time.

Self-Bailer – A raft with a laced-in floor, allowing the water to flow in and out of the boat. Bailing is not needed.

Self-Rescue – When a raft flips, the rower rescues herself by flipping the boat right side up on her own, getting back on the boat, and back in the rower's seat. If the rower is washed out or tipped off the raft, she skips the first step and climbs back on board to start rowing again.

Sun Shower – A two- to five-gallon durable plastic bag that is black on one side with a nozzle at one end, usually clipped to the outside of a gear pile for sun exposure during the day. It heats water when the black side is exposed to the sun. Buy one in sports stores.

Swamper – Low man or woman on the totem pole when it comes to working on a commercial river trip. Swampers help load and unload the boats, assist in setting up camp, and go for whatever the cooks or captains need. A good swamper usually advances up the chain of command.

Sweep – Refers to the last boat in a line of rafts or catarafts. The sweep is usually an experienced boater who can assist in situations where another craft may need assistance (e.g., when a boat flips or someone gets launched out of a raft).

Taco – When a raft folds over on itself. This occasionally happens in big rapids and can be dangerous for people in the raft.

Takeout – The end point of a river trip or where the boats are taken out of the river.

Tammies – Short for tamarisk, an invasive shrub that grows all along the banks of Colorado Plateau rivers. The Bureau of Land Management has invested in a variety of tamarisk eradication efforts, with varying results.

The Canyon – An abbreviation of the Grand Canyon. Apparently, California boaters refer to The Canyon, while western rafters refer to The Grand . . . not sure about the rest of the country.

The Grand – another abbreviation of the Grand Canyon.

Tongue – Often as a rafter drops into a rapid, the approach is over a smooth strip of water that drops into the rapid. It is shaped like a tongue – wider upstream at the top and narrowing as it enters the rapid.

Trip Leader – The person in charge of the trip, often the permit holder. Her word is the final law. Treat her with the utmost of respect.

W – Wind. It's bad luck to say the word out loud, thus the abbreviation.

Z-drag – A system of ropes and pulleys used to right flipped rafts or drag them off rocks.

Appendix II
River Etiquette:
A River Princess Does It Right

Martha Hut
The "Other" Martha

Martha's niece, Rachel, was the inspiration for this guide and for the name "The Other Martha." You can guess that origin. Rachel was 16 years old at the time and had never been on a river trip.

Rivers are where my soul resides. I love all the river's aspects: wild rapids, calm, lazy water, swirling eddies, the changing landscape, sunset, sunrise, reflections, wildlife, the challenges, the simple life, the camaraderie.

Through this little guide I wish to share my experiences on rivers with other women who want to be part of the river. Consider these tips to be guidelines, or river etiquette, if you will.

Peeing on the river

Women go upstream cause skirts go up. Men go downstream cause pants go down.

For southwestern U.S. rivers:

- Pee in the river or in its waterline.

- Fast way #1: Slide your pants crotch to the side and pee. Splash with river water.

- Fast way #2: Stand or squat in the river. No clothing adjustment is required. The river rinses everything.

- On the boat
#1: Hang off the back of the boat. HOLDING ON TIGHT, slide your crotch to the side and pee. RELIEF!
#2: In a self-bailing or open cataraft, pee in the floor. (Be prepared for companions' comments.)
#3: Ask to pull to shore. Other boats will stop to observe the wildlife they assume you must have seen.

- At night use a pee bucket and empty it into the river in the morning.

For other U.S. rivers ask your guide/trip leader discretely.

- Do NOT pee in the river. Instead go 100 feet away from any stream.

- Fast way: Slide your pants crotch to the side and pee, then shake your butt to remove the excess.

- Carry TP with you. After use, put it in a plastic baggie and then put in the trash or burn it in the campfire.

Pooping on the river

For U.S. rivers:

- Most US rivers require that all feces be carried out. This is usually done in a self-contained system that has a toilet seat with the container under it. The container has many names: groover, thunder mug, shitter. Listen carefully at the beginning of your trip so that you use the proper name.

- Try not to pee in the feces container. That's difficult for ladies, but try...

- On southwestern rivers insist that the groover is near the water. On other rivers insist that there is a pee bucket next to the groover. Then you can pee and return to the groover easily.

- Insist that the groover has a beautiful view.

On other rivers ask your guide/trip leader discretely.

Dressing on the river

- Clothes are for warmth, staying dry, for swimming, and for protection from the sun.
- Take your oldest and worst clothes on river trips.
- Mismatched clothes are the best. You may win "Worst Dressed Night" without even trying!

Be respectful of local customs in foreign countries and adjust your wardrobe accordingly.

Getting rid of river clothes

- Sell them to your companions.
- Turn them into rags.
- Leave them behind for the locals to wear.
- Burn them in honor of the river gods.
- Save them for the next river trip – but wash them first!

Bathing on the river

- For heaven sakes, bring a sun shower! Bathing is a ritual. It's meant to be enjoyed.

- Be sure your sun shower is packed on the top of the dunnage, black side up. Explain to nonbelievers that this is the most important piece of equipment to go down the river.

- Use only biodegradable soap, shampoo, and conditioner.

- Never bathe in a side stream.

- Clothes are optional while you're bathing, depending upon the dynamics of your group.

For southwestern U.S. rivers:

- Bathe in or close to the river.

- Select a spot with a deep eddy and a tree or overhanging rock from which to hang your sun shower. Improvise when perfect conditions are not available. You can hang your shower off rocks or off the back of a boat.

- Soap and shampoo in the river. Scream as needed if the water is cold.

- Rinse using your solar shower. Without a solar shower, rinse in the river.

For other U.S. rivers:

- Bathe 100 feet away from the river or any side stream.

- With a sun shower: Select a spot with a tree or overhanging rock from which to hang your sun shower. Submerge in the river. Run to the bathing area and apply soap and shampoo. Rinse with your warm sun shower. Oh, what a luxury!

- Without a sun shower: Fill a bucket with water from the river and haul it to your bathing spot. Submerge in the river. Run to the bathing area and apply soap and shampoo. Rinse by pouring water from the bucket over you. (It is nice to have a helper pour the water over you.) Screaming, once again, may be appropriate.

- Either way: Dry off with the sun or a towel. Apply lotion and put on your clothes. You and your companions will be so GLAD that you have performed this ritual!

On other rivers be respectful of local customs.

Taking care of your feet on the river

- Treat your feet with the greatest of respect. They are much needed equipment on the river. No one wants to have to carry your stuff or do your chores because you were dumb enough to mess up your feet.

- Always wear river sandals or shoes while on the river.

- Put on lots of sunscreen. Burned feet are the worst.

- Give your feet a little extra attention at the end of the day. Before you slip into your sleeping bag, massage them with lotion.

Eating on the river

- Forget all your Amy Vanderbilt training and remember that anything goes.

- Okay, there is one Amy Vanderbilt rule to follow: Wash your hands before eating.

- Hungry women are just as hungry as hungry men. Men don't get to go first. If there seems to be any doubt on the trip, elbow your way to the front of the line and dig in. No sexism is allowed on the river.

- But do be a little bit considerate. There are no supermarkets on the river if you run out of food! Don't take more than you can eat. However, the object is to get rid of the food, so don't be shy. Who wants to keep carrying all that weight on their boat? Well, maybe in the groover!?

- Don't drop your food on the ground because (a) you get less and (b) it creates problems with ants.

- Pick up all food micro trash and put it in the trash.

Dishes and utensils:

- On some trips dishes and utensils are part of the kitchen and on others you bring your own. If you forgot your fork or spoon, two small sticks work nicely as chopsticks. Hands can also be used for eating. (Eating a steak with your hands is very efficient.)

- Wash utensils and dishes using the four-bucket system: Pre-wash, soapy wash, rinse, bleach water soak.

- Bowls can work as cups and vice versa.

- Frisbees can be dishes.

- The river is the place for invention. If you need to, you'll find something that works.

167

Foreign items in your food

- Sand in your food is a common occurrence on a river trip. Do not overreact. Sand provides minerals and is nutritious. It will be a part of your diet on a river trip. The same applies for small bugs.

- On a southwestern river trip, do become alarmed if you suspect that a mouse has been in your food. In a raging dance, throw out all the contents of your dry box and wherever else you suspect the mouse has been. Hantavirus can kill you.

Getting in and out of the boat

In:

- On land, coil up the rope (untie it first) as directed by your boat captain. Brace yourself and hold on to the boat tightly if it is in swift water.

- Be sure you're going to make it into the boat before making your leap. Your captain does not want to have to haul your sorry ass out of the water and into the boat.

- A graceful entry is more becoming but if you must lunge, crawl, scramble, or bumble into the boat, go for it. Do whatever works.

Out:

- When your captain tells you, untie the rope and be prepared to leap to shore.

- Look before you leap. If the shoreline is deep, you may sink to the bottom causing your captain great consternation. She will have to retrieve you AND maneuver the boat.

- Brace yourself and hold on tightly to the rope. If you drop it, you're on shore and out of luck because the rest of your party just went downstream!

- Tie the boat to a non-yielding tree or rock. A good captain will always check your knot and what you tied the boat to. Don't be insulted.

Respecting the cooler

- Ice is what keeps the cooler cold. Ice cannot be made or bought on river trips. Sometimes it can be traded with another party using river booty, but you may not have anything the other party wants.

- Before leaving on your trip find out what you can put-in the cooler. If possible, freeze it beforehand.

- Remember every time you open the cooler ice is lost.

- Only open a cooler with your boat captain's permission. Opening a cooler without permission can cause your captain's wrath to descend upon you.

Avoiding water fights

- Choose a boat captain who does not like water fights.

- Carry things on your boat that cannot get wet – something the whole group does not want to get wet, such as lunch.

- Develop a condition that doesn't allow you to get wet. For example, wear a hearing aid or develop a skin rash.

- Steal everyone's water fighting weapons and hide them on your boat.

- Hide behind others on your boat to avoid getting wet.

- If all else fails, maintain your own loaded arsenal of water guns so that you are more prepared than they are.

Lounging on the river

- For many, a camp chair is a priority piece of equipment.

- Bring your own. Have your trip leader check it out to be sure whoever must pack it won't be cursing you every morning.

- Trip leaders and boat captains get priority use of chairs. Hey, who's getting you and your stuff down the river anyway?

- If you don't have a chair, use an upside-down bail bucket, a log, or a rock. Practice your flexibility and squat. Be creative.

- Do not sit on a life jacket. That reduces its longevity.

Partying on the river

- Arrange your party area so that no one falls in the river and disappears while everyone else is having a hilarious time.

- However, be close enough to the river so that pee breaks may be easily taken.

- Do not destroy the environment while you're partying.

- Keep the cooks entertained and well provided for during party time. Bring them a cocktail or glass of wine.

- Remember the most important river rule – what happens on the river, stays on the river!

Repairing damaged equipment

- Duct tape, duct tape, duct tape. Carry lots of it with you.

- Your captain will have a repair kit to take care of raft repairs, and lots of duct tape.

Becoming your trip leader's best friend

- Remember to help, help, help. There is much work to be done on a river trip. Trip leaders love participants who pitch in, especially those who don't need to be told what to do.

- Volunteer for putting up the groover and taking it down. It's a job that no one wants but it's really not that bad!

- Help out in the kitchen before and after meals.

- Help to load and unload the boats every day.

- Compliment your trip leader. Call her things like omnipotent trip leader, oh great one, leader of the pack. You get the idea.

- Give her special treats. A cocktail at the end of a hard day will be much appreciated.

- Treat her boat with the greatest of respect. It is her castle. Everything has its special place. Always ask where to put things, including yourself and your stuff. Check before helping to tie on the dunnage. Every boater has her own way of doing things and may or may not welcome new ideas.

- Smile, smile, smile. Even though it's a lot of hard work, the trip leader hopes you're having as great a time as she is.

Hiking on the river

- If it's hot, dip your shirt in the river before starting, or submerge your entire body, clothes and all.

- Carry water.

- Carry a phone, camera, binoculars, and other nice-to-have stuff if you don't mind extra weight.

- Wear river sandals or hiking shoes, depending upon the terrain.

- Watch out for rattlesnakes and bears.

- Enjoy, enjoy, enjoy!

Appendix III
A Few River Runner Recipes

Compiled by Kelly Robinson
Submitted by Ellen Delacruz

Mondo Bizarro Sauce
Mollie Katzen, *Moosewood Cookbook*
Martha Hut's standard river meal

- 4 lg cloves garlic
- 1/3 C fresh basil
- 1/3 C minced parsley
- 1 lb bunch spinach, stemmed
- ½ C pinenuts
- 3 med tomatoes
- ½ C Parmesan cheese grated
- ½ t salt
- Freshly ground pepper to taste

At home, place garlic, basil, parsley, spinach, pinenuts, and tomatoes in a blender or food processor and work into a uniform paste. Add tomatoes and process just a few seconds longer. On the river, heat the mixture, then transfer it to bowl and stir in cheese, salt and pepper. Serve with pasta.

Gado Gado
One of Martha's river recipes
(6 servings)

All ingredients can be prepared in advance and served warm or at room temp.

- Assortment of vegetables such as broccoli, green beans, cabbage, carrots, mung bean sprouts, cooked or raw
- Spinach, for creating a bed on the bottom
- Yellow rice to layer onto the spinach (2 cups rice cooked in 3 cups water with ½ tsp. turmeric)
- Tofu and/or hard boiled eggs, sliced or chopped

Peanut sauce

- 1 C creamy peanut butter with 4 T cider vinegar
- 1 heaping T grated ginger
- 2 T soy sauce
- 1 heaping T minced ginger
- 1 t salt
- 3 T brown sugar
- Crushed red pepper to taste
- 1 ½ C hot water
  At home, put everything in the blender and puree. On the river, drizzle over spinach, rice, tofu, eggs, and veggies.

Final toppings (as you wish)

- 2 T sliced ginger,
- 1 C minced onion,
- 12 sliced cloves garlic sautéed in 3 T peanut oil
- Shredded, unsweetened coconut
- Crushed red pepper
- Slices of fruit such as lemons, limes, oranges, apples, pineapple

174

Thai Fish Curry
Yummly.com
A Janette Diegel special

- 1 1/2 lb. white fish
- 3 T red Thai curry paste (divided)
- 2 T coconut oil
- 1/2 medium onion (finely minced)
- 2 T finely minced ginger
- 3 cloves garlic (finely minced)
- 15 oz. coconut milk
- 1/2 C water
- 1 T fish sauce
- 1 T coconut sugar
- 4 C veggies (chopped, pictured are green beans, carrots, and red bell peppers)
- Cilantro
- Lime juice
- Chicken or shrimp optional

Saute onions, garlic, and ginger for big-time flavor. Now create the sauce by adding coconut milk, curry paste, fish sauce (stinky but tasty!), a little coconut sugar. Now some chopped veggies go into the pot to cook for a few minutes. Add the fish last as it cooks very quickly.

For a slaw: Chop some cabbage and add mint with Thai basil and carrots, or fruit. I like apple and kale.

Salad dressing:

- 2 chili peppers, diced
- 3 cloves garlic
- 2 T sugar
- 1 T rice vinegar
- 3 T fresh lime juice
- 2 T fish sauce
- 3 T vegetable oil

Ratatouille
Zan's fresh-from-the-garden dish
(6-8 servings)

Easy to prepare ahead of time and simply warm up for a river dinner.

- 5 large cloves garlic, roughly chopped
- 1 large onion, sliced
- Peppers (the equivalent of 2-3 green or red peppers, but use whatever's in the garden), cored, seeded, and chopped
- 6 medium tomatoes (I prefer Romas) peeled, cored and cut into pieces
- 3 medium Japanese eggplants, cut into 1/2-inch-thick rounds
- 3 medium zucchini, cut into 1/2-inch-thick rounds
- Whatever else is in the garden that looks good, like green beans*
- 1/4 packed C parsley roughly chopped
- 1/4 packed C basil roughly chopped
- Salt and pepper to taste
- Extra virgin olive oil as needed

Sauté garlic and onion in the olive oil first, then add the other veggies except the tomatoes and sauté them. Peel the tomatoes by plunging them into boiling water for 20-30 seconds, then squeeze the extra juice out of them, and add them to the mixture. Simmer a little while until it looks good. Serve over rice or noodles with Parmesan and some good bread. ENJOY the bounty of summer!

*If I'm using green beans, I cook them a little first.

176

Nat's Superduper Salmon Sauce
An end-of-trip favorite from Martha

- 1 bottle sun dried tomato Alfredo sauce
- 1 can canned salmon
- 1 can mushrooms
- Pimentos
- Capers
- 1 jar roasted red peppers
- Oil, garlic, salt, pepper
- Pasta (penne works well on the river) or rice

Sauté mushrooms, peppers, capers, and pimentos in oil and garlic. Add salmon and sauce. Salt and pepper to taste. Serve over pasta or rice.

Deconstructed Tamales
Zan's latest addition to the river menu (6-8 servings)

Pre-prepare everything and freeze in gallon bags.

1 to 1 ½ tubes of polenta. Break apart into a mixing bowl. Using a mixer, add enough water to make the polenta creamy. Freeze in a gallon bag.

Saute:
· 1 16 oz package of mushrooms, sliced
· 1 onion, chopped
· 1 red, orange or yellow pepper, sliced

Throw in:
· 2 sm cans diced chilies
· 2-3 cans Rotele tomatoes with green chilies - drained
· 1 can corn - drained
· 1 can black beans - drained
· 2-3 Tbsp tomato paste to hold everything together

Season with:
· A lot of chili powder
· A little cumin
· Salt
· Pepper
· A hint of garlic

Freeze in another gallon bag.

For the "meatatarians," get a pound of seasoned chicken or pork at the local taco place and serve it on the side.

Warm everything up. Serve with polenta on the bottom, then the mixture, and, if desired, meat.

Top with:
· Guac
· Sour cream
· Grated cheese

Curry Stand Chicken with Tikka Masala Sauce
(6 servings)
AllRecipies.com
Beth Booton's specialty

- 2 T ghee (clarified butter)
- 1 onion, finely chopped
- 4 cloves garlic, minced
- 1 T ground cumin
- 1 t salt
- 1 t ground ginger
- 1 t cayenne pepper
- 1/2 t ground cinnamon
- ¼ t ground turmeric
- 1 14-ounce can tomato sauce
- 1 C heavy whipping cream
- 2 t paprika
- 1 T white sugar
- 1 T vegetable oil
- 4 skinless, boneless chicken breast halves, cut into bite-size pieces
- ½ t curry powder
- ½ t salt or to taste
- 1 t white sugar or to taste

Directions

- Heat ghee in a large skillet over medium heat and cook and stir onion until translucent, about 5 minutes. Stir in garlic; cook and stir just until fragrant, about 1 minute. Stir cumin, 1 t salt, ginger, cayenne pepper, cinnamon, and turmeric into the onion mixture; fry until fragrant, about 2 minutes.
- Stir tomato sauce into the onion and spice mixture, bring to a boil, and reduce heat to low. Simmer sauce for 10 minutes, then mix in cream, paprika, and 1 T sugar. Bring sauce back to a simmer and cook, stirring often, until sauce is thickened, 10 to 15 minutes.

179

- Heat vegetable oil in a separate skillet over medium heat. Stir chicken into the hot oil, sprinkle with curry powder, and sear chicken until lightly browned but still pink inside, about 3 minutes; stir often. Transfer chicken and any pan juices into the sauce. Simmer chicken in sauce until no longer pink, about 30 minutes; adjust salt and sugar to taste.

River Tacos
Nancy Hess's satisfying dinner

- Sauté garlic and onion until sweaty.
- Add one can refried beans and one can plain beans (any will do). Put in a bowl.
- Cook chorizo. Put in a bowl.
- Cut cabbage, cheese, tomatoes, jalapenos, and other fixins, and put in separate bowls.

Heat corn tortillas.

Serve with shredded cheese, sour cream, a couple of different salsas, and guacamole.

Have everyone construct tacos to their liking.

River Key Lime Pie
Zan's recipe adapted from the back of a *Nellie and Joe's Key Lime Juice* bottle

- 1 pre-made graham cracker crust

In a bowl combine

- ½ cup *Nellie and Joe's Key Lime Juice*
- 1 can sweetened condensed milk

Stir vigorously and watch the magic happen. When well blended and thick, pour into the pie shell. Let the pie sit for a while. Put it in a cooler if there's room. Serve with canned whipped cream.

Acknowledgments
Zan Merrill

This compilation is truly a group effort. It would be excessive to individually acknowledge the contributions of each author, much as I would like to. My sincere thanks goes out to all of them and to everyone who encouraged us along the way.

When the idea for this book first popped into my mind, it was the fall of 2021. A group of us was camped on a beautiful ledge in the middle of the Goosenecks of the San Juan River sipping cocktails and thinking about making dinner. A single man floated by eyeing us curiously and hollered, "Where are your men?" We cracked up, and the idea was born.

In the days that followed, as we all were sharing our river stories, I conceived my plan to compile a collection. The five other ladies were all in and helped make a list of about 35 women who might be willing to contribute to a book of women's river stories. I hounded the women on the list terribly for the next three months, determined to get this thing off the ground. By mid-January I had a piece or two from every one of the 20-some women who had agreed to write something. I am truly grateful for their stories. They also sent me hundreds of priceless photos. They were beautiful, interesting, and many had historic value. I wish I could have included them all.

Initial editing would not have progressed as well as it did without Janette Diegel's writing and editing expertise. Admittedly rough, our first compilation nevertheless garnered the interest of a small publisher, so off it went. Five months passed before the manuscript was rejected. Nikki Naiser, formerly a professional book editor, teamed up with me to do some heavy-handed editing and rewriting, including a complete reorganization. We submitted the updated manuscript to a regional university press. The acquisitions editor graciously invested a considerable amount of time to offer clear direction, but our compilation did not meet the academic standards of the university press. However, with the benefit of his valuable input, we went back to the drawing board with more editing, rewriting, and reorganizing. Janette did a final editorial pass, and the result is what you see.

We hope you like *Where Are Your Men?* well enough to tell your friends because now that we've self-published, advertising and marketing are up to us. We appreciate any help you can give. Thank you!

For more info:
WhereAreYourMen.com

www.ingramcontent.com/pod-product-compliance
Lightning Source LLC
Chambersburg PA
CBHW062133040426

42335CB00039B/2084